Prentice Hall

MATHEMATICS
Course 3

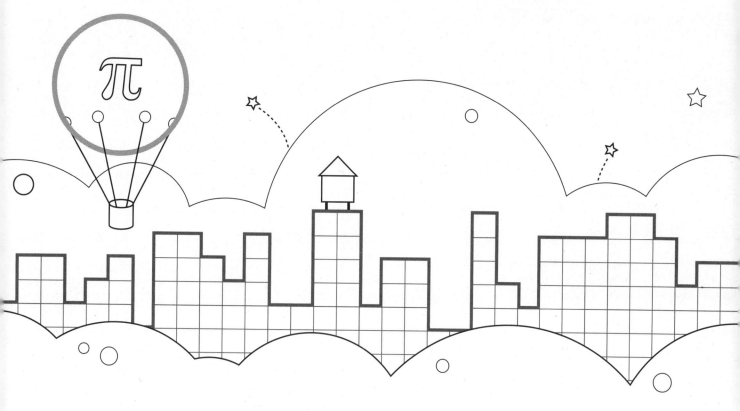

Progress Monitoring
Assessments

Boston, Massachusetts • Chandler, Arizona • Glenview, Illinois • Upper Saddle River, New Jersey

ISBN-13: 978-0-13-372197-3
ISBN-10:   0-13-372197-3

4 5 6 7 8 9 10 V016 13 12 11

Table of Contents

To the Teacher:

During the school year, you assess how students are learning in your classroom using various types of assessments. Prentice Hall's *Progress Monitoring Assessments* provides a clear path to adequate yearly progress through systematic testing and recommendations for remediation.

Formative Assessments

When you give tests that help you identify students' strengths and weaknesses, your assessments are considered formative assessments. The results of these tests serve as a guide in planning and adjusting curriculum to assist struggling students and enhance all students' learning. There are several assessments and related activities in this book to assist you.

Screening Test

Before launching into the curriculum, you need to know how well your students read and how proficient they are in basic computation and problem-solving skills. Use the Screening Test to measure student readiness for your course.

Benchmark Tests

Proficiency testing is at the heart of progress monitoring and student achievement. At specified intervals throughout the year, give Benchmark Tests to evaluate student progress toward mastery of essential content.

Test-Taking Strategies Practice

Since a critical factor of assessment is to provide opportunities for students to learn better, use the Test-Taking Strategies Practice pages to investigate problem-solving strategies and strengthen students' application of these strategies with problems of varying complexity.

Standardized Test Practice

Since the NAEP, SAT 10, ITBS, and TerraNova tests are common assessments at high school, use these pages to acquaint students with topics, question formats, and practice. The activities and practice provided on these pages will allow students to be less anxious when they take these high stakes assessments for evaluation purposes.

Summative Assessments

When you give tests, usually at the end of a quarter or year, and the goal of the assessment is to evaluate mastery, your assessments are considered summative assessments. There are several assessments and related activities in this book to assist you. Quarter Tests, Mid-Course Tests, and Final Tests are available at two levels. The regular levels are designed to measure mastery of content over a span of chapters with the rigor presented in the lessons and exercises of the Student Edition. The below level forms are provided to support less-proficient readers, beginning English-language learners, and other struggling students. The problems meet the same mastery of content, but contain more visual support and fewer problems.

Assessment Support

Providing clear and supportive feedback to students is critical to progress monitoring, so use the comprehensive reports and answer keys provided in this book to map student results and follow-up with relevant remediation assignments.

Screening Test

1. What is the place value of the underlined digit?

    1,503.<u>2</u>3

    A hundredths

    B tenths

    C tens

    D hundreds

2. Which number is equivalent to *eighteen and four hundredths*?

    A 18,400

    B 18.400

    C 18.040

    D 18.004

3. Which fraction is less than $\frac{5}{7}$?

    A $\frac{10}{14}$

    B $\frac{4}{5}$

    C $\frac{3}{4}$

    D $\frac{3}{5}$

4. Add.

    17,503 + 370 + 2,568

    A 19,341

    B 19,431

    C 20,431

    D 20,441

5. Maryanne saved $63,720 for her retirement. Her husband saved $38,350. How much did they save altogether?

    A $25,370

    B $92,070

    C $102,070

    D $102,700

6. Subtract.

    60,020 − 21,989

    A 29,022

    B 38,031

    C 48,041

    D 59,031

7. Add.

    $12\frac{2}{5} + 9\frac{1}{3}$

    A $21\frac{3}{8}$

    B $21\frac{11}{15}$

    C $21\frac{2}{3}$

    D $22\frac{11}{15}$

8. Subtract.

$$8\frac{3}{8} - 5\frac{3}{4}$$

A $2\frac{3}{8}$

B $2\frac{5}{8}$

C   3

D $3\frac{3}{8}$

9. Add.

$$22.013 + 8.09$$

A   30.103

B   30.220

C   30.913

D   31.030

10. Subtract.

$$23.05 - 18.2$$

A   4.85

B   5.30

C   5.35

D   41.25

11. Multiply.

$$125 \times 63$$

A   1,115

B   7,865

C   7,875

D   7,965

12. Divide.

$$1,782 \div 18$$

A   11

B   33

C   66

D   99

13. There are 936 people in line to get onto a ferryboat. Each ferry holds the same number of people. If each ferryboat can hold 12 people, how many boats are needed to transport all of the people?

A   36 boats

B   78 boats

C   7,480 boats

D   11,232 boats

14. A soccer team won 15 games and lost 6 games. What is the ratio of the team's wins to games played?

A   2 to 5

B   5 to 7

C   2 to 7

D   5 to 2

15. Which number is *not* an odd number?

A   17,231

B   15,123

C   13,310

D   12,321

16. Which number is a factor of 210?

   A 4

   B 7

   C 8

   D 11

17. Which is an example of the Identity Property for Addition?

   A $15 + (-15) = 0$

   B $9 + 6 = 9 + 6$

   C $5 + 0 = 5$

   D $9 \times 0 = 0$

18. You measure the height, the width and the length of a box. What measurement can you find using all three measurements?

   A mass

   B girth

   C length

   D capacity

19. When measuring the capacity of a fish tank, which unit of measure cannot be used?

   A cubic centimeter

   B square meter

   C ounce

   D liter

20. The perimeter of a rectangle is given by the formula $2l + 2w = P$, where l = length and w = width. A gardener wants to edge with a picket fence a garden that measures 16 meters wide and 10 meters long. How many meters of fence does the gardener need?

   A 26 meters

   B 36 meters

   C 52 meters

   D 160 meters

21. A kitchen floor measures 9 feet by 12 feet. The owner wants to lay 18-inch by 18-inch ceramic tile to completely cover the floor. How many tiles does the owner need? Use the formula $A = l \times w$.

   A 6 tiles

   B 10 tiles

   C 24 tiles

   D 48 tiles

22. The science class is measuring the length of an earthworm's body. Which unit of measure should the class use?

   A meters

   B grams

   C centimeters

   D kilometers

23. Which of the following shapes does *not* describe the figure?

A polygon

B rectangle

C trapezoid

D quadrilateral

24. Which angle measures approximately 45°?

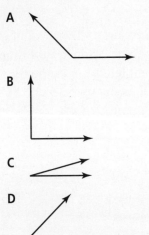

A

B

C

D

25. Which statement is true?

A All triangles have one right angle.

B All right triangles have 3 right angles.

C All acute triangles have 3 acute angles.

D All obtuse triangles have 3 obtuse angles.

26. Which two-dimensional shapes make up the bases of the solid shown?

A squares

B triangles

C rectangles

D trapezoids

27. A company sells running shoes at a discount. Their catalog lists the regular price and the discount price. Which type of display would best help a person compare the regular price and the discount price?

A spreadsheet

B double bar graph

C double line graph

D two circle graphs

28. If 185 students participate in extra-curricular activities, how many play soccer?

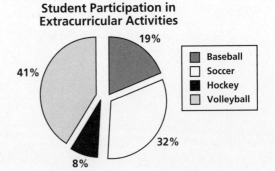

Student Participation in Extracurricular Activities

19%

41%

32%

8%

Baseball
Soccer
Hockey
Volleyball

A 19 students

B 32 students

C 60 students

D 75 students

29. In the school cafeteria, students can choose from 3 different fruits, 6 different drinks, and 2 different main courses. How many different combinations are there to choose from?

A 11

B 12

C 18

D 36

30. The letters of the word ATLANTIC are placed in a bag. What is the probability that a consonant (letters that are not vowels) will be picked from the bag?

A $\frac{3}{8}$

B $\frac{1}{2}$

C $\frac{5}{8}$

D 1

31. What is the next number in the pattern?

5, 9, 17, 33, 65, …

A 68

B 75

C 98

D 129

32. Solve.

$$m + 45 = 137$$

A $m = -182$

B $m = -92$

C $m = 92$

D $m = 182$

33. Solve.

$$-3x + 2 = -13$$

A $x = -13$

B $x = -5$

C $x = -3\frac{2}{3}$

D $x = 5$

34. A technician charges a $50 estimation fee and then $25 per hour to repair washing machines. Write an equation for the total cost of the technician's service, C, if the technician works h hours.

A $C = 50 + 25h$

B $h = 50 + 25C$

C $C = 25 + 50h$

D $C = 75h$

35. Which point is represented by the ordered pair $(-4, 2)$?

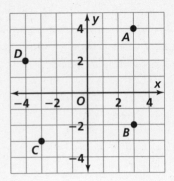

A A

B B

C C

D D

36. Which number is a solution of $y \leq 4$?

A 4

B 4.01

C 4.5

D 5.25

Benchmark Test 1

1. Simplify $24 \div (8 - 2) + 3 \cdot 4$.

  A 13

  B 16

  C 18

  D 26

2. What is the value of this expression if $m = 4$ and $k = 2$?

$$m \cdot \left(7k - \frac{20}{m}\right)$$

  F 16

  G 20

  H 36

  J 51

3. A bus leaves a station that is 357 miles from Chicago and travels toward Chicago at a rate of 50 miles per hour. Which expression represents the distance of the bus from Chicago after n hours?

  A $357 + 50n$

  B $357 - 50n$

  C $357n - 50$

  D $357n + 50$

4. Which list shows the numbers $15, -26, 10$, and -2 in order from least to greatest?

  F $-2, 10, 15, -26$

  G $-26, 15, 10, -2$

  H $-2, -26, 10, 15$

  J $-26, -2, 10, 15$

5. During one play of a football game, a football team lost 5 yards. Which point on the number line below represents this situation?

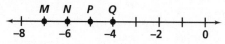

  A M

  B N

  C P

  D Q

6. Which expression has the greatest value?

  F -9

  G $|-12|$

  H $-|-15|$

  J $|14 - 3|$

7. Evaluate $16 - x + y$ for $x = -3$ and $y = -4$.

  A 9

  B 15

  C 17

  D 21

8. An airplane, flying at an altitude of 15,000 feet above sea level, flies directly above a submarine that is traveling at a depth of 1,250 feet below sea level. What is the distance between the airplane and the submarine?

F 13,750 ft

G 14,750 ft

H 15,250 ft

J 16,250 ft

9. A diver descends 64 feet in 8 seconds. What is the diver's average change in depth per second?

A −16 feet per second

B −8 feet per second

C 8 feet per second

D 16 feet per second

10. Which property is shown by the equation below?

$$-3.2 + 6.8 = 6.8 + (-3.2)$$

F Identity Property

G Associative Property

H Distributive Property

J Commutative Property

11. Which expression uses the distributive property to find $6 \cdot 4.97$?

A $6(5) - 0.30$

B $6(5 - 0.30)$

C $6(5 - 0.03)$

D $6(5) - 0.03$

12. Lisa bought 6 paintbrushes that cost $2.97 each. What was the total cost of the paintbrushes?

F $17.70

G $17.82

H $18.70

J $18.82

13. The number of visitors in April to a city science museum was 3 times as many as the number of visitors in March. If 1,270 people visited the museum in April, which equation can be used to find the number of visitors (v) in March?

A $1,270v = 3$

B $3 + v = 1,270$

C $3v = 1,270$

D $1,270 + v = 3$

14. Solve $\frac{m}{4} = -1.5$.

F −6

G −5.5

H 2.5

J 5

15. During the first week that tickets were on sale for a symphony performance, 285 tickets were sold. There are 345 tickets still available for the performance. Use the equation $t - 285 = 345$ to find the original number of tickets (t) available for the performance.

A 60

B 285

C 345

D 630

16. What is the simplest form of the fraction $\frac{66}{156}$?

    F $\frac{11}{26}$

    G $\frac{22}{51}$

    H $\frac{33}{76}$

    J $\frac{17}{39}$

17. Rachel needs 10 ounces, or $\frac{5}{8}$ pound, of cheese for a recipe. Which of the following is equivalent to the amount of cheese Rachel needs?

    A 0.125 pound

    B 0.16 pound

    C 0.58 pound

    D 0.625 pound

18. The repeating decimal $0.\overline{27}$ is equivalent to what fraction?

    F $\frac{27}{100}$

    G $\frac{3}{11}$

    H $\frac{2}{7}$

    J $\frac{9}{11}$

19. Which list of numbers is ordered from least to greatest?

    A $-\frac{2}{9}, -0.22, 0.1, \frac{2}{3}$

    B $-0.22, -\frac{2}{9}, 0.1, \frac{2}{13}$

    C $-0.22, -\frac{2}{9}, \frac{2}{13}, 0.1$

    D $0.1, -0.22, \frac{2}{13}, -\frac{2}{9}$

20. Which value of n makes the following statement true?

$$\frac{3}{5} < n$$

    F $\frac{7}{12}$

    G $\frac{8}{15}$

    H $\frac{11}{15}$

    J $\frac{14}{25}$

21. For which of these values of x will the expression $\frac{x-4}{x}$ have the greatest value?

    A -10

    B -4

    C 4

    D 10

22. There are $3\frac{3}{4}$ cups of flour, $1\frac{1}{2}$ cups of sugar, $\frac{2}{3}$ cup of brown sugar, and $\frac{1}{4}$ cup of oil in a cake mix. How many cups of ingredients are there in all?

F $4\frac{1}{2}$ cups

G $5\frac{1}{6}$ cups

H $5\frac{1}{2}$ cups

J $6\frac{1}{6}$ cups

23. In a toy box, $\frac{1}{4}$ of the toys are dolls, $\frac{2}{5}$ of the toys are puzzles, and the rest are cars and trucks. What fraction of the toys are cars and trucks?

A $\frac{7}{20}$

B $\frac{1}{3}$

C $\frac{13}{20}$

D $\frac{2}{3}$

24. What value of t makes the following equation true?

$$3\frac{1}{8} + t = -\frac{3}{4}$$

F $-3\frac{7}{8}$

G $-2\frac{3}{8}$

H $2\frac{3}{8}$

J $3\frac{7}{8}$

25. Topsoil sells for $2.48 per cubic foot. How much does $10\frac{1}{2}$ cubic feet of topsoil cost?

A $4.23

B $12.98

C $20.48

D $26.04

26. Two thirds of the girls at a summer camp like to jump rope. If 162 girls attend the camp, how many like to jump rope?

F 54

G 62

H 108

J 243

27. Simplify the following expression.

$$\frac{1}{2}\left(\frac{3}{5} \div \frac{7}{8}\right)$$

A $\frac{21}{80}$

B $\frac{12}{35}$

C $\frac{24}{35}$

D $\frac{35}{48}$

28. Which expression has a value of 144?

F $2^3 \cdot 3^3$

G $3^4 \cdot 4^3$

H $2^4 \cdot 3^2$

J $3^2 \cdot 4^3$

29. Evaluate $-t^2 + (5 - t)^3$ for $t = 3$.

A -3

B -1

C 15

D 17

30. The formula for the volume of a cube is $V = s^3$, where s is the length of a side. What is the volume of a cube with sides of length 5 meters?

F 10 cubic meters

G 25 cubic meters

H 125 cubic meters

J 625 cubic meters

31. Which of the following shows 4,630,000 written in scientific notation?

A 4.63×10^4

B 4.63×10^5

C 4.63×10^6

D 4.63×10^7

32. Which number is the greatest?

F 4.7×10^4

G 3.1×10^5

H 4.02×10^5

J 3.65×10^4

33. At the point in the moon's orbit when it is nearest the Earth, the distance from the moon to the center of the Earth is about 2.22×10^5 miles. What is this distance written in standard form?

A 22,200 miles

B 222,000 miles

C 2,220,000 miles

D 22,200,000 miles

34. A train traveled 357 miles in $8\frac{1}{2}$ hours. What was the train's average rate of speed?

F 29 miles per hour

G 30 miles per hour

H 42 miles per hour

J 45 miles per hour

35. The formula for converting degrees Fahrenheit to degrees Celsius is $C = \frac{5}{9}(F - 32)$. If the temperature is 68°F, what is the temperature in degrees Celsius?

A 20°C

B 36°C

C 56°C

D 65°C

36. The formula for the area of a trapezoid is $A = \frac{1}{2}h(b_1 + b_2)$. Solve this formula for b_1.

F $b_1 = \frac{A}{2h} + b_2$

G $b_1 = \frac{A}{2h} - b_2$

H $b_1 = \frac{2A}{h} + b_2$

J $b_1 = \frac{2A}{h} - b_2$

Benchmark Test 2

1. What are the coordinates of point *F*?

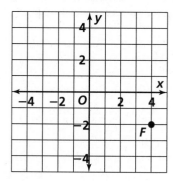

   A $(-4, -2)$

   B $(-2, -4)$

   C $(-2, 4)$

   D $(4, -2)$

2. In which quadrant of the coordinate plane is the point $(-3, 7)$ located?

   F I

   G II

   H III

   J IV

3. What are the coordinates of the point 4 units to the left of and 6 units above the point $(3, -2)$?

   A $(-4, -4)$

   B $(-1, 4)$

   C $(7, 8)$

   D $(9, -6)$

4. Which of the following ordered pairs is a solution to the equation $y = -3x$?

   F $(-9, 3)$

   G $(3, 9)$

   H $(6, -18)$

   J $(18, -6)$

5. Which of the following ordered pairs is a solution of the linear equation graphed below?

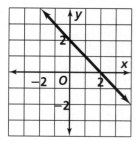

   A $(-2, 3)$

   B $(-1, 3)$

   C $(0, -2)$

   D $(1, -1)$

6. Which table of values was used to create the following graph?

F

x	−3	−1	0	1
y	−2	−1	2	4

G

x	−3	−2	0	1
y	4	2	2	4

H

x	−3	−1	0	1
y	−4	0	2	4

J

x	−3	−2	0	1
y	−3	−2	2	4

7. A vendor is selling pumpkin pies at a farmer's market. The graph below shows the relationship between the number of pies sold and the vendor's income and expenses. How many pies must the vendor sell in order to break even?

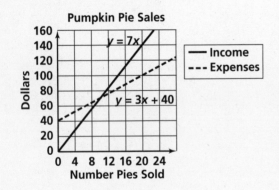

Pumpkin Pie Sales

A 10

B 20

C 40

D 70

8. What is the solution of the following system of equations?

$$y = 2x$$
$$y = x - 4$$

F $(-4, -8)$

G $(0, -4)$

H $(2, 4)$

J $(4, 0)$

9. A student group is selling T-shirts for $10 each. The group buys the shirts for $5 each and spends a total of $50 to have a picture of the school mascot printed on them. How many shirts must the students sell in order to break even?

A 10

B 20

C 100

D 200

10. How many lines of symmetry does a square have?

F 1

G 2

H 4

J 8

11. Which of the following words has a horizontal line of symmetry?

A BID

B CAB

C MOW

D TIE

12. The figure shown below has rotational symmetry. What is the angle of rotation?

F 50°

G 72°

H 75°

J 120°

13. What are the coordinates of the image of $T(3, -5)$ after it is reflected across the x-axis?

A $(-3, -5)$

B $(-3, 5)$

C $(3, -5)$

D $(3, 5)$

14. The image of point B after a counterclockwise rotation of 90° about the origin is $B'(-2, 4)$. What are the coordinates of point B?

F $(-4, -2)$

G $(-4, 2)$

H $(4, -2)$

J $(4, 2)$

15. Line $A'B'$ is a translation of line AB. Which rule describes this translation?

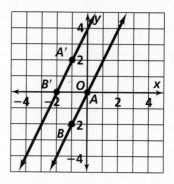

A $(x, y) \rightarrow (x - 1, y + 2)$

B $(x, y) \rightarrow (x + 1, y - 2)$

C $(x, y) \rightarrow (x + 2, y - 1)$

D $(x, y) \rightarrow (x + 2, y + 2)$

16. Which of the following is the closest estimate of $\sqrt{85}$?

F 5

G 8

H 9

J 10

17. Which of the following is *not* an irrational number?

A π

B $0.345345345 \ldots$

C $0.212112111 \ldots$

D $\sqrt{7}$

18. What is the positive square root of $\frac{16}{100}$?

F $\frac{2}{25}$

G $\frac{4}{25}$

H $\frac{2}{5}$

J $\frac{4}{5}$

19. A basket of fruit contains 6 apples, 4 oranges, and 8 bananas. What is the ratio of bananas to apples in the basket?

A $\frac{2}{3}$

B $\frac{3}{4}$

C $\frac{4}{3}$

D $\frac{3}{2}$

20. Which of the following jars of peanut butter represents the best buy?

F a 10-ounce jar for $2.36

G a 12-ounce jar for $2.52

H a 16-ounce jar for $2.64

J a 20-ounce jar for $3.50

21. Ms. Lanier has $2,400 to invest in a stock. Stock A is selling for $40 per share, and Stock B is selling for $30 per share. How many more shares can she buy if she invests in Stock B instead of Stock A?

A 20

B 60

C 80

D 100

22. A leaky faucet wastes 2 quarts of water per hour. At this rate, how many gallons of water will the faucet waste per day?

F 12 gallons per day

G 24 gallons per day

H 48 gallons per day

J 96 gallons per day

23. The longest river in the world is 5,584 kilometers in length. The second longest river is 4,007 kilometers in length. What is the difference, in meters, between the lengths of these two rivers?

A 1,577 meters

B 15,770 meters

C 157,700 meters

D 1,577,000 meters

24. The speed of light is about 186,000 miles per second. What is the speed of light in feet per minute?

F 52 feet per minute

G 272,800 feet per minute

H 11,160,000 feet per minute

J 58,924,800,000 feet per minute

25. Which pair of ratios forms a proportion?

A $\frac{1}{9}$ and $\frac{9}{81}$

B $\frac{2}{5}$ and $\frac{8}{40}$

C $\frac{2}{3}$ and $\frac{3}{8}$

D $\frac{7}{8}$ and $\frac{14}{15}$

26. Solve the following proportion for *b*.

$$\frac{3.5}{4.2} = \frac{b}{12}$$

F   10

G   11.3

H   14

J   14.4

27. Travis needs $\frac{2}{3}$ cup of blueberries to make a batch of 12 muffins. How many cups of blueberries will he need to make 90 muffins?

A   5 cups

B   8 cups

C   60 cups

D   72 cups

28. The two triangles shown below are similar. What is the value of *x*?

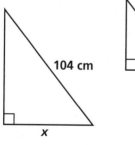

F   25.6 centimeters

G   65 centimeters

H   166.4 centimeters

J   204 centimeters

29. In order to measure the width of a river, two park rangers made the measurements shown below. If the triangles in the diagram are similar, what is the width, *w*, of the river?

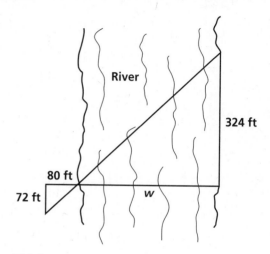

A   292 feet

B   316 feet

C   332 feet

D   360 feet

30. A 32-foot flagpole casts a 150-foot-long shadow. At the same time, a nearby tree casts a 30-foot long-shadow. What is the height of the tree to the nearest foot?

F   5 feet

G   6 feet

H   141 feet

J   160 feet

31. A state map has a scale of 1 inch : 8 miles. If the length of a road on the map is 16 inches, what is the actual length of the road?

A   2 miles

B   24 miles

C   88 miles

D   128 miles

32. The dimensions of a model ship are $\frac{1}{60}$ of the dimensions of the actual ship. If the model's deck is 12 inches long, what is the length of the actual deck?

  F   50 inches

  G   72 inches

  H   500 inches

  J   720 inches

33. The door on a model car is 5 centimeters long. The length of the actual car door is 1.4 meters. What is the scale of the model?

  A   1 centimeter : 0.28 meter

  B   1 centimeter : 0.9 meter

  C   1 centimeter : 3.6 meters

  D   1 centimeter : 7 meters

Benchmark Test 3

1. Last year, 23% of all cars sold by a car dealer were blue. How is this percent written as a decimal?

   A 0.023

   B 0.23

   C 2.3

   D 23.0

2. Fifteen percent of the students at a school ride the bus. What fraction of the students ride the bus?

   F $\frac{1}{15}$

   G $\frac{3}{20}$

   H $\frac{1}{5}$

   J $\frac{3}{10}$

3. Three fifths of Gina's books are mysteries. What percent of Gina's books are mysteries?

   A 3.5%

   B 6.0%

   C 35%

   D 60%

4. What is 76% of 528?

   F 143.94

   G 353.76

   H 401.28

   J 694.74

5. Cordelia buys a CD priced at $12.95. If the sales tax rate is 8%, how much sales tax does she pay?

   A $0.62

   B $1.04

   C $1.20

   D $1.62

6. On Saturday, a movie theater had total sales of $32,400.00. The theater's concession stand had sales of $13,186.80. What percent of the theater's total sales came from the concession stand?

   F 14.5%

   G 24.6%

   H 40.7%

   J 68.6%

7. Sixty players tried out for a school football team in 2002. In 2003, only 48 players tried out for the team. What was the percent of decrease in the number of players trying out for the team?

   A 12%

   B 20%

   C 25%

   D 80%

8. In January, the price of a dozen eggs at a grocery store was $0.89. By June, the price had increased to $0.99. What was the percent of increase in the price, to the nearest tenth of a percent?

F 9.0%

G 10.0%

H 10.1%

J 11.2%

9. At the beginning of the school year, there were 6 fish in the life science aquarium. At the end of the school year, there were 42 fish in the aquarium. What was the percent of increase in the number of fish?

A 60%

B 70%

C 600%

D 700%

10. A video game that regularly costs $29.95 is on sale for 15% off. What is the sale price of the video game?

F $25.46

G $28.38

H $29.50

J $34.44

11. A jewelry store marks up the price of a topaz ring 215%. If the ring cost the store $70.00, what is the selling price of the ring?

A $91.50

B $150.50

C $161.50

D $220.50

12. Inez buys a pair of boots on sale for $32.20. The sale price is 20% off the regular price. What is the regular price of the boots?

F $34.20

G $38.64

H $40.25

J $57.96

13. Laura deposits $1,500 in an account with a simple interest rate of 6% per year. How much interest will the account earn in 3 years?

A $90

B $180

C $270

D $300

14. Ben deposits $320 in an account that earns 3.5% simple interest per year. What is the balance in the account after 4 years?

F $322.80

G $331.20

H $364.80

J $432.00

15. A business invests $25,000 in an account that earns 5% interest compounded annually. What is the balance in the account after 2 years?

A $25,062.50

B $26,250.00

C $27,500.00

D $27,562.50

16. A litter of kittens includes 3 gray ones, 3 white ones, and 2 black ones. What is the probability that a kitten chosen at random is either gray or white?

F $\frac{1}{3}$

G $\frac{1}{2}$

H $\frac{2}{3}$

J $\frac{3}{4}$

17. A tray contains 12 ham sandwiches, 10 turkey sandwiches, and 8 peanut butter sandwiches. If Carrie takes a sandwich from the tray at random, what is the probability that she takes a ham sandwich?

A 8%

B 12%

C 40%

D 67%

18. Leo rolls two number cubes, each with faces numbered 1 to 6. What is the probability that the numbers rolled have a sum of 5?

F $\frac{1}{18}$

G $\frac{1}{9}$

H $\frac{1}{6}$

J $\frac{1}{4}$

19. Solve $-5 + \frac{x}{-3} = 28$.

A -99

B -89

C -79

D -69

20. A sound studio charges a $52 reservation fee and $26 per hour. Felipe paid a total of $130 to use the sound studio. Which equation can be used to find the total number of hours (h) during which Felipe used the studio?

F $26 + 52h = 130$

G $52 + 26h = 130$

H $52(26 + h) = 130$

J $26(h + 52) = 130$

21. To make a beaded necklace Jaime bought a bag containing 24 silver beads and 3 bags of colored beads. Each bag of colored beads contained the same number of beads. Jaime bought a total of 78 beads to make the necklace. How many beads were in each bag of colored beads?

  A 18

  B 26

  C 50

  D 54

22. Simplify the following expression.

$$4(6y - 5) - (3y + 9)$$

  F $21y - 29$

  G $21y + 4$

  H $25y - 11$

  J $25y + 14$

23. Posters cost p dollars each and CDs cost c dollars each. Eric bought 2 CDs and 1 poster and his brother bought 1 CD and 3 posters. Which expression represents the total cost of the items?

  A $c + 2p$

  B $2c + p$

  C $3c + 4p$

  D $4c + 3p$

24. The owner of a clothing store is shipping an order of shirts and pants to a customer. The shirts weigh x ounces each and the pants weigh $x + 7$ ounces each. Which expression represents the total weight of the shipment if it contains 4 shirts and 2 pairs of pants?

  F $6x + 7$

  G $6x + 14$

  H $13x$

  J $13x + 7$

25. Solve $8(c - 5) - 3c = 15$.

  A 4

  B 5

  C 11

  D 15

26. Solve $2 - 4p = -4 - 6p$.

  F -3

  G -1

  H 2

  J 5

27. Adriana spent 15 hours volunteering at an animal shelter this month. This is 3 more than twice the number of hours she volunteered last month. How many hours did Adriana volunteer last month?

  A 6

  B 7

  C 9

  D 12

28. A family of two adults and two children invite some of the children's friends to go to a movie. Adult admission is $7.50, and children's admission is $6.50. The total admission cost for the group is $47.50. Which equation can be used to find x, the number of friends with the family at the movie?

F $2(\$7.50) + \$6.50 + x = \$47.50$

G $2(\$7.50) + \$6.50(2 - x) = \$47.50$

H $2(\$7.50) + \$6.50(2 + x) = \$47.50$

J $2(\$7.50) + 2(\$6.50) + x = \$47.50$

29. A hiker leaves on Trail A at 7:00 A.M. traveling 3 mph. A second hiker leaves on the same trail at 8:30 A.M. traveling 6 mph. What time will the second hiker catch up to the first?

A 9:30 A.M.

B 10:00 A.M.

C 10:37 A.M.

D 11:43 A.M.

30. A father and his daughter together weigh seven times the daughter's weight x. The father weighs 180 lbs. Which equation can be used to find the daughter's weight?

F $180 - 7x = x$

G $x - 180 = 7x$

H $x + 7x = 180$

J $180 + x = 7x$

31. Solve $4m < -32$.

A $m < -256$

B $m > -256$

C $m < -8$

D $m > -8$

32. The graph below represents the solution to which inequality?

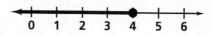

F $x - 3 \le 7$

G $x + 5 \le 9$

H $x - 1 \ge 3$

J $x + 6 \ge -2$

33. Tamara is planting bushes around her house. So far today she has planted 5 bushes and she wants to plant at least 12 bushes today. Which inequality can be used to find the number of bushes (b) Tamara still needs to plant?

A $b + 5 \ge 12$

B $b - 5 \ge 12$

C $5b \ge 12$

D $\frac{b}{5} \ge 12$

34. Solve $3.4x - 5.1 < 10.2$.

F $x < 1.5$

G $x < 2.1$

H $x < 4.5$

J $x < 8.1$

35. Solve $18 + \dfrac{n}{-3} > 21$.

A $n < -9$

B $n < -81$

C $n > -9$

D $n > -81$

36. A team of four students is participating in an academic competition. The team's score for the competition is the average of the number of points earned by each member of the team. The points earned by three members of the team are 20, 23, and 22. What is the least number of points the fourth student can earn if the team needs a score of at least 22 to advance to the next round?

F 20

G 21

H 22

J 23

STOP

Benchmark Test 4

1. In the diagram below $m\angle 3 = 52°$. What is the measure of $\angle 2$?

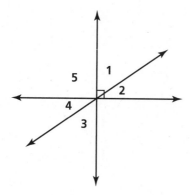

A 28°

C 42°

B 38°

D 52°

2. Refer to the figure to determine which of the following statements is *not* true.

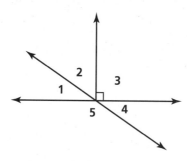

F Angle 1 and angle 4 are vertical angles.

G Angle 2 and angle 3 are complementary angles.

H Angle 3 and angle 4 are adjacent angles.

J Angle 4 and angle 5 are supplementary angles.

3. A plumb bob is a device that consists of a weight suspended from a string. Due to the force of gravity, when the plumb bob is at rest it hangs perpendicular to the ground. When it is at rest, what type of angle does the plumb bob form with the ground?

A right

C obtuse

B acute

D straight

4. In the diagram below, which pair of angles are alternate interior angles?

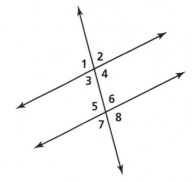

F $\angle 1$ and $\angle 5$

H $\angle 4$ and $\angle 5$

G $\angle 2$ and $\angle 7$

J $\angle 6$ and $\angle 8$

5. In the diagram below $a \parallel b$. What is $m\angle 1$?

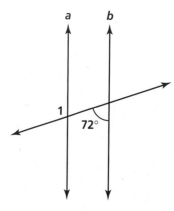

A 36°

C 108°

B 72°

D 144°

6. In the diagram below, m ∥ n and a ∥ b. Which pair of angles are *not* corresponding angles?

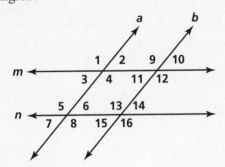

F ∠1 and ∠5

G ∠3 and ∠11

H ∠6 and ∠14

J ∠9 and ∠15

7. In the diagram below, ABCD ≅ FGHI. Which statement is *not* true?

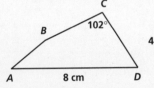

A AB = 3 cm   **C** m∠D = 34°

B FI = 8 cm   **D** m∠H = 102°

8. By which method is the pair of triangles below congruent?

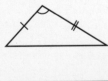

F Side-Side-Side

G Side-Angle-Side

H Angle-Side-Angle

J Angle-Angle-Angle

9. Which triangle is congruent to the triangle below by the Angle-Side-Angle method?

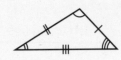

A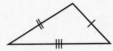

B

C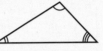

D

10. What is the best classification for the triangle below?

F equilateral acute

G equilateral obtuse

H isosceles acute

J isosceles obtuse

11. What is the name for a quadrilateral with exactly one pair of parallel sides?

A rhombus   **C** trapezoid

B rectangle   **D** parallelogram

12. Which name does *not* describe the figure?

F square   **H** trapezoid

G rhombus   **J** parallelogram

13. Which regular polygon has interior angles that each measure 135°?

   A triangle   **C** octagon

   B pentagon   **D** decagon

14. Benzene is a chemical compound used in the manufacture of products such as plastics and detergents. It is composed of six carbon atoms in the shape of a regular hexagon, as shown below. What is the sum of the angles inside the "benzene ring"?

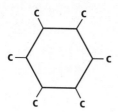

   F 180°   **H** 540°

   G 360°   **J** 720°

15. A carpenter is building a deck in the shape of a pentagon with two right angles. The remaining three angles are congruent, as shown below.

What is value of n?

   A 45   **C** 108

   B 60   **D** 120

16. What is the circumference of a circle with a diameter of 12 inches? Use 3.14 for π.

   F $C = 18.84$ in.

   G $C = 37.68$ in.

   H $C = 75.36$ in.

   J $C = 113.04$ in.

17. A circular pond has a circumference of 50.24 feet. What is the area of the pond?

   A 157.76 ft^2

   B 200.96 ft^2

   C 401.92 ft^2

   D 803.84 ft^2

18. What is the area of the shaded region to the nearest tenth of a square centimeter?

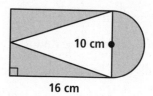

   F 119.3 cm^2

   G 158.5 cm^2

   H 199.3 cm^2

   J 238.5 cm^2

19. What type of solid is shown below?

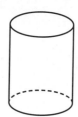

   A cylinder   **C** pyramid

   B cone   **D** prism

20. Which term *best* describes the part labeled $\overline{FG}$ in the solid shown below?

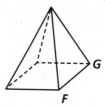

   F radius   **H** base edge

   G diameter   **J** lateral face

21. Which pair of three-dimensional figures can be combined to create the solid shown below?

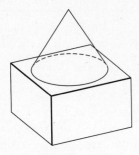

A a rectangular prism and a cone

B a rectangular prism and a pyramid

C a triangular prism and a cone

D a triangular prism and a rectangular prism

22. What solid can be formed from the net shown below?

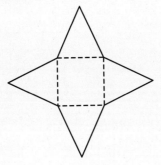

F cone

G prism

H pyramid

J cylinder

23. What combination of shapes makes up the net of a cylinder?

A 1 circle and 1 rectangle

B 1 circle and 2 rectangles

C 2 circles and 1 rectangle

D 2 circles and 2 rectangles

24. Which two nets will form triangular prisms?

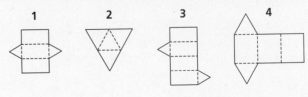

F 1 and 3

G 1 and 4

H 2 and 3

J 3 and 4

25. Find the surface area of the cylinder shown below to the nearest square millimeter. Use 3.14 as an approximation for π.

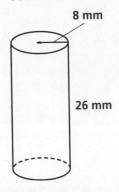

A 402 square millimeters

B 854 square millimeters

C 1,306 square millimeters

D 1,708 square millimeters

26. What is the surface area of the prism shown below?

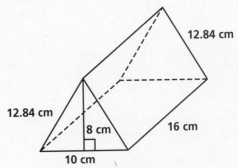

F 80 square centimeters

G 160 square centimeters

H 410.88 square centimeters

J 650.88 square centimeters

27. Rita stores birdseed in a cylindrical metal container with a diameter of 11 inches and a height of 15 inches. What is the surface area of the container to the nearest square inch? Use 3.14 as an approximation for π.

A 129 square inches

B 449 square inches

C 612 square inches

D 708 square inches

28. What is the volume of the prism shown below?

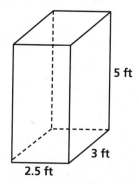

F 7.5 cubic feet

G 37.5 cubic feet

H 43.75 cubic feet

J 187.5 cubic feet

29. What is the volume of the prism shown below?

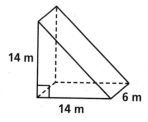

A 98 cubic meters

B 588 cubic meters

C 1,176 cubic meters

D 1,372 cubic meters

30. A cylinder has a volume of approximately 2,034 cubic inches and a radius of 6 inches. What is the best approximation of the height of the cylinder?

F 12 inches

G 16 inches

H 18 inches

J 22 inches

31. What is the volume of the figure shown below to the nearest tenth of a cubic foot?

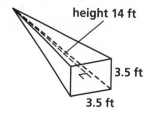

A 57.2 cubic feet

B 85.75 cubic feet

C 171.5 cubic feet

D 514.5 cubic feet

32. What is the volume of the cone shown below? Use 3.14 as an approximation for π.

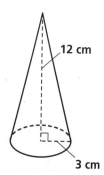

F 113.04 cubic centimeters

G 169.56 cubic centimeters

H 226.08 cubic centimeters

J 339.12 cubic centimeters

33. What is the volume of the figure shown below to the nearest cubic centimeter? Use 3.14 as an approximation for π.

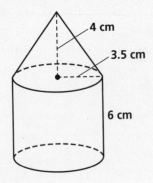

A 77 cubic centimeters

B 103 cubic centimeters

C 231 cubic centimeters

D 282 cubic centimeters

34. If each dimension of Prism B is half the corresponding dimension of Prism A, which of the following statements is true?

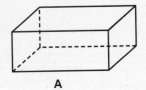

F The surface area of Prism B is half the surface area of Prism A.

G The surface area of Prism B is one-third the surface area of Prism A.

H The surface area of Prism B is one-fourth the surface area of Prism A.

J The surface area of Prism B is one-eighth the surface area of Prism A.

35. The cylinders shown below are similar. What is the ratio of the surface area of the larger cylinder to the surface area of the smaller cylinder?

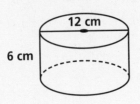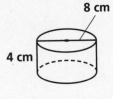

A $\frac{3}{2}$

B $\frac{2}{1}$

C $\frac{9}{4}$

D $\frac{4}{1}$

36. The cylinders shown below are similar. What is the volume of Cylinder A to the nearest cubic meter?

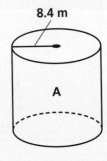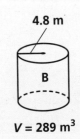

$V = 289 \text{ m}^3$

F 506 cubic meters

G 885 cubic meters

H 1,158 cubic meters

J 1,549 cubic meters

Benchmark Test 5

1. Which of the following should the manager of a car dealership use to determine the most popular type of car sold by the dealership?

   A mode

   B mean

   C range

   D median

2. The number of points scored by a basketball team during the first 8 games of the season is shown below. What is the mean number of points scored for these games?

   65, 58, 72, 74, 82, 67, 75, 71

   F 70.5

   G 71.5

   H 78

   J 82

3. The table below shows the monthly mean air temperatures for the months of November through April at a weather station on Lake Superior. What is the median of these temperatures?

   Lake Superior Temperatures

Month	Mean Air Temperature (C°)
November	4
December	−4
January	−7
February	−6
March	−1
April	2

   A −6.5

   B −5.5

   C −2.5

   D −2.0

4. The line graph below shows how the earnings of a company have changed over time. Which of the following best explains why this graph could be misleading?

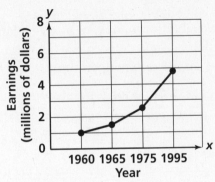

F The intervals of the horizontal scale are unequal.

G The earnings are given in millions of dollars.

H The horizontal scale does not start at zero.

J The graph does not have a key.

5. The bar graph below shows the attendance at a yearly school fund-raiser. Which statement is not supported by the data presented in the graph?

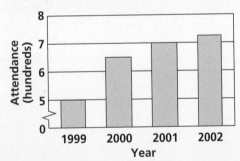

A About 25 more people attended in 2002 than in 2001.

B The attendance in 2002 was nearly 50% greater than in 1999.

C The greatest increase in attendance was between 1999 and 2000.

D The attendance in 2001 was about three times the attendance in 1999.

6. The table below shows the deer population in a state park over a period of several years.

Deer Population

Year	Number of Deer
1999	531
2000	508
2001	483
2002	457
2003	492

Danielle plans to make a line graph of the data in the table. Which of the following scales for the axis showing number of deer would be most likely to give the impression that the deer population has changed very little over time?

F multiples of 10 from 450 to 540

G multiples of 20 from 400 to 600

H multiples of 25 from 300 to 550

J multiples of 50 from 0 to 550

7. Of 30 students, 10 take drama, 8 take art, and 12 take music. Of the students taking art, 5 also take music. Of the students taking drama, 4 also take music. No student takes all three classes. How many students take only music?

A 0

B 3

C 9

D 12

8. The Capitol Hill Jazz Band has 16 members. Seven members play both brass and woodwind instruments. Six members play both percussion and brass instruments. None of the members play all three kinds of instruments. If 3 members play only woodwind instruments, how many members play both woodwind and percussion instruments?

F   0

G   3

H   5

J   8

9 At a county fair, 12 children play the ring toss game or the dart game. Suppose 9 children play the ring toss game and 7 children play the dart game. Of those 7 children, 3 play only the dart game. How many children play only the ring toss game?

A   3

B   5

C   7

D   9

10. What is the difference between the median and the mode of the data shown in the stem-and-leaf plot?

Stem	Leaves
3	0 1 3 3
4	0 5 6
5	1 3 5 5 6
6	2 4 4 4
7	0 1 4

Key: 3|4 means 34.

F   0

G   9

H   55

J   64

11. The list below shows the ages of 12 tortoises. Which box-and-whisker plot correctly represents this set of data?

68, 74, 78, 72, 54, 84, 78, 79, 38, 96, 99, 102

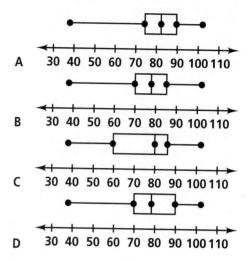

12. A company has an annual budget of $1,000,000. How much more of its annual budget does the company spend on wages than on materials?

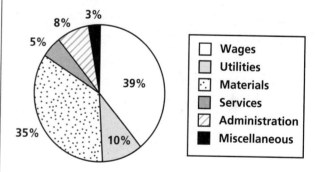

F $20,000

G $40,000

H $200,000

J $290,000

13. A new ride has opened at an amusement park. The histogram below shows the number of children in each age group who rode the ride on its first day of operation. About how many children went on the ride on the first day?

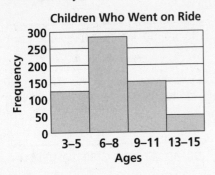

Children Who Went on Ride

A 100

B 300

C 600

D 1,200

14. The bar graph below shows the number of videos rented from a video store over a five-month period. About how many more videos were rented in March than in January?

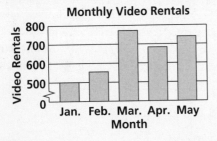

Monthly Video Rentals

F 175

G 275

H 500

J 600

15. The line graph below shows the number of acres of cantaloupes and watermelons planted in the United States between 1998 and 2002. In what year was the difference between the number of acres planted with cantaloupes and the number of acres planted with watermelons the least?

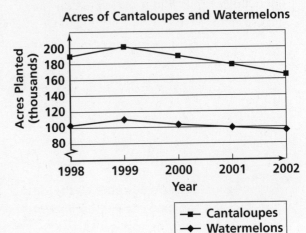

Acres of Cantaloupes and Watermelons

A 1998

B 1999

C 2001

D 2002

16. Look at the stem-and-leaf plot shown below. What do the stem 5 and the leaf 3 represent?

Length of Flat Worms
(in centimeters)

```
4 | 0 1 2 3 3
5 | 1 3 5 5 6
6 | 0 1 2
7 | 1
```

Key: 4|0 means 4.0 cm.

F 0.53 cm

G 5.03 cm

H 5.3 cm

J 53 cm

17. Look at the box-and-whisker plot shown below. What is the median of the set of data represented by the plot?

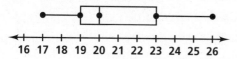

16 17 18 19 20 21 22 23 24 25 26

A 19

B 20

C 21

D 26

18. The members of the student council are creating a circle graph to show their yearly budget. They plan to spend 65% of the budget on the class picnic. What is the measure of the central angle that represents this section of the graph?

F 65°

G 126°

H 234°

J 300°

19. What type of trend is shown by the scatter plot below?

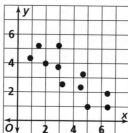

A negative

B none

C opposite

D positive

20. A scatter plot comparing students' ages and the color of their eyes would most likely show which type of trend?

F negative

G none

H opposite

J positive

21. For which topic would a scatter plot of the data most likely show a positive trend?

A amount of rainfall and number of water-rationing days

B time spent training for a race and time needed to finish a race

C number of snacks eaten and amount of time spent exercising

D number of workers in a factory and the amount of goods produced

22. Kaitlin wants to show how the number of students at her school has changed over time. Which type of display would be most appropriate for this purpose?

F circle graph

G line graph

H box-and-whisker plot

J stem-and-leaf plot

23. Miguel has put together a list of the heights of 50 professional basketball players. He wants to display the data in a way that will make it easy to determine the median height of the players. Which type of display would be most appropriate for this purpose?

A box-and-whisker plot

B circle graph

C line graph

D scatter plot

24. In which situation would a circle graph most likely be an appropriate way to display the set of data?

F to show the average high temperature in 5 cities

G to show how the heights of 3 children change with age

H to show the results of a survey of 100 people about their favorite vegetable

J to show the percent of households in 10 states that own more than one telephone

25. Of 4,000 seeds that a grower plants, 3,447 germinate. Find *P*(planted seed will germinate). Round to the nearest percent.

A 11%

B 27%

C 74%

D 86%

26. Which of the following is an example of theoretical probability?

F You attempt 15 free throws during a basketball game and make 8 of them.

G You play a game with your friend and win 3 out of 5 times.

H A clock manufacturer makes random checks of its clocks. Of 500 inspected, 15 are defective.

J You roll a number cube and the probability of rolling a 3 is 1 out of 6.

27. A town of 20,000 people takes a survey to find out how many people want a new library. Of 1,500 people surveyed, 900 want a new library. Using the survey results, predict the total number of people in the town who want a new library.

A 900

B 1,000

C 6,000

D 12,000

28. At a particular factory, the probability of a water pump being defective is $\frac{1}{85}$. In a shipment of 2,975 water pumps, how many are likely to be defective?

F 35

G 45

H 65

J 85

29. A cube is labeled with the colors red, yellow, green, orange, blue, and purple. When the cube is tossed, the probability of getting each color is $\frac{1}{6}$. Predict how many times you will get the color orange if you toss the cube 90 times.

  A 6

  B 15

  C 30

  D 36

30. You spin a four-colored spinner 9 times. The results are red once, green three times, blue once, and yellow four times. In 70 spins, predict the total number of times the result will be green.

  F 8

  G 11

  H 17

  J 23

31. Which survey does not use a random sample?

  A Customers in one music store are surveyed to find out which radio station is most popular in the town.

  B Customers in a store are surveyed to find out their satisfaction with the store's service.

  C Students in a school cafeteria are surveyed to find out their favorite candidates for student elections.

  D Participants in a book club are surveyed to find out which books are their favorites.

32. Which question is not biased?

  F Which music artists do you prefer listening to?

  G Do you like entertaining computer games or dull books?

  H Do you like your tea with lemon or milk?

  J Do you prefer walking in a city park or walking in the beautiful, serene countryside?

33. Sonia and James are conducting a survey to find out which extracurricular activities are the most popular among students at their school. Which group of students should they survey if they want a random sample?

  A Mr. Callaway's 4th period drama class

  B All of the students on the soccer team

  C All of the students at a school assembly

  D All of the students in the orchestra

34. Twenty cards are numbered 1–20. You draw a card, return it to the deck, and then draw a second card. Find P(even, then 7).

  F $\frac{1}{10}$

  G $\frac{11}{20}$

  H $\frac{1}{40}$

  J $\frac{17}{40}$

35. There are 8 loose socks in a drawer. Six are black, and two are blue. You select a sock at random from the drawer. Without replacing the first sock, you select a second sock. Find P(black, then black).

  A $\frac{3}{4}$

  B $\frac{2}{7}$

  C $\frac{7}{16}$

  D $\frac{15}{28}$

36. Which event is not an independent event?

  F You select a card from a deck of cards. Without replacing it, you select another card.

  G You select a marble from a bag. You return the marble to the bag and draw another one.

  H You spin a spinner twice. The pointer stops in two different places.

  J You roll three number cubes, and the numbers rolled are 5, 6, and 2.

37. Five friends are going to a movie. In how many different seating lineups can the friends sit in the theater?

  A 25

  B 60

  C 120

  D 200

38. Simplify. $_{11}P_4$

  F 110

  G 990

  H 7,920

  J 55,440

39. There are 23 projects in Division 4 at the science fair. Awards will be given for first, second, and third places. How many different arrangements of three winners are possible?

  A 46

  B 506

  C 1,012

  D 10,626

40. Simplify. $_6C_3$

  F 6

  G 20

  H 60

  J 120

41. A store offers 18 toppings for a pizza. How many different three-topping pizzas can you choose?

  A 51

  B 816

  C 1,836

  D 4,896

42. Coach Collins must choose five of the 20 swimmers on the local swim team to participate in the district competition. How many different groups of five can she choose?

  F 90

  G 1,965

  H 15,504

  J 372,096

STOP

Quarter 1 Test

Chapters 1–3

Form A

1. Evaluate $x(4 + 5y)$ for $x = 3$ and $y = 2.4$.

2. A company sells its product for $16 per unit. How many units would have to be sold in order for the company to earn $528?

3. Compare. Write $<$, $>$, or $=$.

   $|11| \underline{\quad?\quad} |{-13}|$

4. Jared hiked from 132 feet above sea level to 6 feet below sea level. Write an integer to express the difference in these elevations.

5. Evaluate the expression $\dfrac{13}{-30 - a}$ for $a = -4$.

6. Simplify. $8 + 9 - 2^3$

7. Evaluate the expression $3x^3 + 5$ for $x = -2$.

8. Simplify. $-4(m - 6)$

9. Simplify. $(-22)(18 - 7)$

10. Rewrite this expression using exponents.

    $3 \cdot 3 \cdot 3 \cdot 3 \cdot x \cdot x \cdot x \cdot y \cdot y$

For Exercises 11–13, solve each equation.

11. $15 = x + 26$

12. $\dfrac{n}{4} = 11$

13. $7p = -105$

14. Simplify. $5x + 8(x - 5)$

15. Write the composite numbers in the list below.

    $37, 43, 47, 26, 32, 2, 17, 40, 16$

16. Find the GCF of 35 and 90.

17. Explain how to write the fraction $\frac{81}{108}$ in simplest form.

18. Sam was at bat 20 times and had 14 hits. Write his batting average as a decimal.

19. Write 1.35 as a mixed number in simplest form.

20. Write $-3\frac{2}{5}$ as a decimal.

21. Write the repeating decimal $0.\overline{4}$ as a fraction in simplest form.

22. Use a factor tree to find the prime factorization of 126.

23. Order $\frac{3}{8}$, -1.25, $-2\frac{4}{5}$, 0.34, -0.63 from least to greatest.

24. Compare. Write $<$, $>$, or $=$. $\quad \frac{3}{16} \underline{\quad?\quad} 0.2$

25. You are making bread that requires $3\frac{1}{2}$ cups of whole wheat flour and $2\frac{1}{2}$ cups of white flour. How many cups of flour is that in all?

26. Subtract. $8\frac{7}{16} - 2\frac{1}{3}$

27. Multiply. $4\frac{1}{2} \times 1\frac{1}{3}$

28. Divide. $3\frac{3}{4} \div 1\frac{1}{2}$

29. Use the formula $P = 2l + 2w$ to find P when $l = 12$ and $w = 7$.

30. Find the length of the hypotenuse.

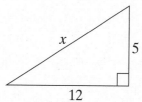

31. Is the triangle with the following dimensions a right triangle?

9 cm, 12 cm, 18 cm

32. Is $\sqrt{18}$ rational or irrational? Explain.

33. Estimate $\sqrt{38}$ to the nearest integer.

34. Graph the ordered pairs in the table. Connect the points to determine if the graph is linear.

x	1	2	3	4	5
y	4	−3	2	−1	0

35. Give the coordinates of a point located in Quadrant IV.

36. Determine whether $(−6, −39)$ is a solution of $y = 5x + 9$.

37. Complete the chart for the equation $y = −2x + 1$.

x	y
2	
4	
6	

38. Graph the equation $y = 2x − 1$.

39. Graph $\triangle PQR$ with $P(0, 7)$, $Q(3, 6)$ and $R(1, 1)$. Then graph the image of a translation 2 units to the left and 4 units down.

40. Graph the triangle whose vertices have the coordinates given below. Then draw its reflection over the x-axis.
$M(−7, 2), N(−1, 2), P(−3, 5)$

41. From Question 40, in which quadrant is the reflection of $\triangle MNP$?

42. From Question 40, how many lines of symmetry does $\triangle MNP$ have?

43. Use the graph below. Tell whether $\triangle B$ is an image of $\triangle A$ after a translation, reflection, or rotation.

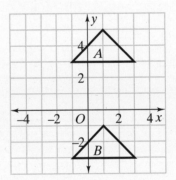

44. How many degrees counterclockwise was figure ABC rotated around the origin?

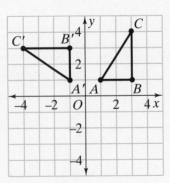

Quarter 1 Test

Chapters 1–3

Form B

1. Evaluate $x(4 + 5y)$ for $x = 4$ and $y = 6.4$.

2. A company sells its product for $12 per unit. How many units would have to be sold in order for the company to earn $504?

3. Compare. Write $<$, $>$, or $=$.

   $|-7| \underline{\ ?\ } |-4|$

4. The temperature fell from 28 degrees above zero to 5 degrees below zero. Write an integer to express the difference in these temperatures.

5. Evaluate the expression $\frac{17}{-57 - a}$ for $a = -6$.

6. Simplify. $15 + 3 - 4^3$

7. Evaluate the expression $4x^3 + 5$ for $x = -2$.

8. Simplify. $-5(m - 3)$

9. Simplify. $20(-6) + 4(-6)$

10. Rewrite this expression using exponents.

    $4 \cdot 4 \cdot 4 \cdot x \cdot x \cdot y \cdot y$

For Exercises 11–13, solve each equation.

11. $11 = y + 13$

12. $\frac{x}{6} = 12$

13. $9w = -81$

14. Simplify. $3x + 7(x - 8)$

15. Write the composite numbers in the list below.
    37   46   23   44   19   33   16   5   50

16. Find the Greatest Common Factor (GCF) of 24 and 56.

17. Explain how to write the fraction $\frac{56}{120}$ in simplest form.

18. Sam was at bat 20 times and had 16 hits. Write his batting average as a decimal.

19. Write 1.95 as a mixed number in simplest form.

20. Write $-2\frac{1}{2}$ as a decimal.

21. Write the repeating decimal $0.\overline{7}$ as a fraction in simplest form.

22. Use a factor tree to find the prime factorization of 360.

23. Order $\frac{4}{5}$, -0.97, $4\frac{3}{5}$, -1.2, 0.90 from least to greatest.

24. Compare. Write $<$, $>$, or $=$. $\frac{2}{3} \underline{\ ?\ } 0.67$

25. To make light blue paint, you add $1\frac{3}{4}$ pt of blue paint to $3\frac{2}{4}$ pt of white paint. How much light blue paint do you have?

26. Subtract. $4\frac{1}{3} - 2\frac{2}{5}$

27. Multiply. $5\frac{1}{2} \times 3\frac{1}{3}$

28. Divide. $4\frac{2}{3} \div 2\frac{1}{2}$

29. Use the formula $V = lwh$ to find V when $l = 10$, $w = 5$, and $h = 6$.

30. Find the length of the hypotenuse.

31. Is the triangle with the following dimensions a right triangle?

9 cm, 12 cm, 15 cm

32. Is $\sqrt{196}$ rational or irrational? Explain.

33. Estimate $\sqrt{50}$ to the nearest integer.

34. Graph the ordered pairs in the table. Connect the points to determine if the graph is linear.

x	1	2	3	4	5
y	4	5	6	7	8

35. Give the coordinates of a point located in Quadrant III.

36. Determine whether $(-4, -5)$ is a solution of $y = 5x + 9$.

37. Complete the chart for the equation $y = -3x + 2$.

x	y
2	
4	
6	

38. Graph the equation. $y = 3x - 2$

39. Graph $\triangle PQR$ with $P(0, 7)$, $Q(3, 6)$, and $R(1, 1)$. Then graph the image of a translation 3 units to the left and 5 units down.

40. Graph the triangle whose vertices have the given coordinates. Then draw its reflection over the x–axis.
$M(-7, 2), N(-1, 2), P(-3, 5)$

41. From Question 40, in which quadrant is the reflection of $\triangle MNP$?

42. From Question 40, how many lines of symmetry does $\triangle MNP$ have?

43. Use the graph below. Tell whether $\triangle A$ is an image of $\triangle B$ after a rotation, reflection, or translation.

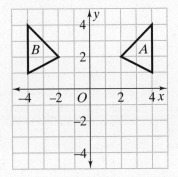

44. How many degrees clockwise was $\triangle ABC$ rotated around the origin?

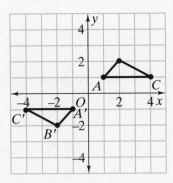

Quarter 1 Test

Form D

Chapters 1–3

1. Evaluate $x(4 + 5y)$ for $x = 3$ and $y = 2.4$.

2. A company sells its product for $16 per unit. How many units would have to be sold in order for the company to earn $528?

3. Compare. Write $<$, $>$, or $=$.

   $|11| \underline{\ \ ?\ \ } |-13|$

4. Jared hiked from 132 feet above sea level to 6 feet below sea level. Write an integer to express the difference in these elevations.

5. Evaluate the expression $\frac{13}{-30 - a}$ for $a = -4$.

6. Simplify. $8 + 9 - 2^3$

7. Evaluate the expression $3x^3 + 5$ for $x = -2$.

8. Simplify. $-4(m - 6)$

9. Simplify. $(-22)(18 - 7)$

For Exercises 10–12, solve each equation.

10. $15 = x + 26$

11. $\frac{n}{4} = 11$

12. $7p = -105$

13. Simplify. $5x + 8(x - 5)$

14. Write the composite numbers in the list below.

    37, 43, 47, 26, 32, 2, 17, 40, 16

15. Find the GCF of 35 and 90.

16. Explain how to write the fraction $\frac{81}{108}$ in simplest form.

17. Sam was at bat 20 times and had 14 hits. Write his batting average as a decimal.

18. Write 1.35 as a mixed number in simplest form.

19. Write the repeating decimal $0.\overline{4}$ as a fraction in simplest form.

20. Use a factor tree to find the prime factorization of 126.

21. Order $\frac{3}{8}, -1.25, -2\frac{4}{5}, 0.34, -0.63$ from least to greatest.

22. Compare. Write $<$, $>$, or $=$.

    $\frac{3}{16} \underline{\ \ ?\ \ } 0.2$

23. You are making bread that requires $3\frac{1}{2}$ cups of whole wheat flour and $2\frac{1}{2}$ cups of white flour. How many cups of flour is that in all?

24. Subtract. $8\frac{7}{16} - 2\frac{1}{3}$

25. Multiply. $4\frac{1}{2} \times 1\frac{1}{3}$

26. Divide. $3\frac{3}{4} \div 1\frac{1}{2}$

27. Use the formula $P = 2l + 2w$ to find P when $l = 12$ and $w = 7$.

28. Find the length of the hypotenuse.

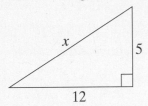

29. Is $\sqrt{18}$ rational or irrational? Explain.

30. Graph the ordered pairs in the table. Connect the points to determine if the graph is linear.

x	1	2	3	4	5
y	4	−3	2	−1	0

31. Give the coordinates of a point located in Quadrant IV.

32. Determine whether $(−6, −39)$ is a solution of $y = 5x + 9$.

33. Complete the chart for the equation $y = −2x + 1$.

x	y
2	
4	
6	

34. Graph $\triangle PQR$ with $P(0, 7)$, $Q(3, 6)$ and $R(1, 1)$. Then graph the image of a translation 2 units to the left and 4 units down.

35. Graph the triangle whose vertices have the coordinates given below. Then draw its reflection over the x-axis.
$M(−7, 2), N(−1, 2), P(−3, 5)$

36. Use the graph below. Tell whether $\triangle B$ is an image of $\triangle A$ after a translation, reflection, or rotation.

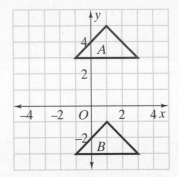

37. How many degrees counterclockwise was $\triangle ABC$ rotated around the origin?

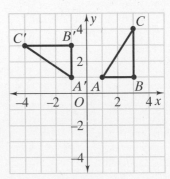

Quarter 1 Test
Chapters 1–3

Form E

1. Evaluate $x(4 + 5y)$ for $x = 4$ and $y = 6.4$.

2. A company sells its product for $12 per unit. How many units would have to be sold in order for the company to earn $504?

3. Compare. Write $<$, $>$, or $=$.

   $|-7|$ __?__ $|-4|$

4. The temperature fell from 28 degrees above zero to 5 degrees below zero. Write an integer to express the difference in these temperatures.

5. Evaluate the expression $\dfrac{17}{-57 - a}$ for $a = -6$.

6. Simplify. $15 + 3 - 4^3$

7. Evaluate the expression $4x^3 + 5$ for $x = -2$.

8. Simplify. $-5(m - 3)$

9. Simplify. $20(-6) + 4(-6)$

For Exercises 10–12, solve each equation.

10. $11 = y + 13$

11. $\dfrac{x}{6} = 12$

12. $9w = -81$

13. Simplify. $3x + 7(x - 8)$

14. Write the composite numbers in the list below.

   37   46   23   44   19   33   16   5   50

15. Find the Greatest Common Factor (GCF) of 24 and 56.

16. Explain how to write the fraction $\dfrac{56}{120}$ in simplest form.

17. Sam was at bat 20 times and had 16 hits. Write his batting average as a decimal.

18. Write 1.95 as a mixed number in simplest form.

19. Write the repeating decimal $0.\overline{7}$ as a fraction in simplest form.

20. Use a factor tree to find the prime factorization of 360.

21. Order $\frac{4}{5}$, -0.97, $4\frac{3}{5}$, -1.2, 0.90 from least to greatest.

22. Compare. Write $<$, $>$, or $=$.

   $\frac{2}{3}$ __?__ 0.67

23. To make light blue paint, you add $1\frac{3}{4}$ pt of blue paint to $3\frac{2}{4}$ pt of white paint. How much light blue paint do you have?

24. Subtract. $4\frac{1}{3} - 2\frac{2}{5}$

25. Multiply. $5\frac{1}{2} \times 3\frac{1}{3}$

26. Divide. $4\frac{2}{3} \div 2\frac{1}{2}$

27. Use the formula $V = lwh$ to find V when $l = 10, w = 5,$ and $h = 6$.

28. Find the length of the hypotenuse.

29. Is $\sqrt{196}$ rational or irrational? Explain.

30. Graph the ordered pairs in the table. Connect the points to determine if the graph is linear.

x	1	2	3	4	5
y	4	5	6	7	8

31. Give the coordinates of a point located in Quadrant III.

32. Determine whether $(-4, -5)$ is a solution of $y = 5x + 9$.

33. Complete the chart for the equation $y = -3x + 2$.

x	y
2	
4	
6	

34. Graph $\triangle PQR$ with $P(0, 7), Q(3, 6)$ and $R(1, 1)$. Then graph the image of a translation 3 units to the left and 5 units down.

35. Graph the triangle whose vertices have the given coordinates. Then draw its reflection over the x–axis.
$M(-7, 2), N(-1, 2), P(-3, 5)$

36. Use the graph below. Tell whether $\triangle A$ is an image of $\triangle B$ after a rotation, reflection, or translation.

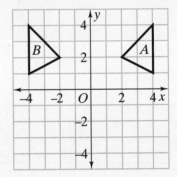

37. How many degrees clockwise was $\triangle ABC$ rotated around the origin?

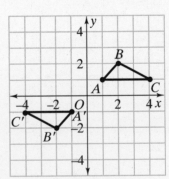

Quarter 2 Test

Chapters 4–6

Form A

1. Find the unit pay rate of $26.50 for 5 hours of work.

2. Find an equal rate.
   44 ft/s = __?__ mi/h

3. Carol found she had a mystery-to-comedy videotape ratio of 8 to 3. If she has 36 comedy tapes in her collection, how many mystery tapes does she have? What is the total number of tapes?

4. Solve. $\frac{18}{q} = \frac{30}{65}$

5. Are the rectangles similar? Explain.

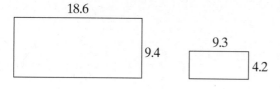

6. The two figures are similar. Find x.

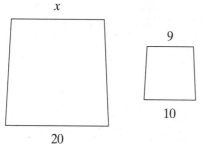

7. For a drawing that requires less detail, an architect has taken the drawing of a building and reduced it. Find the scale factor.

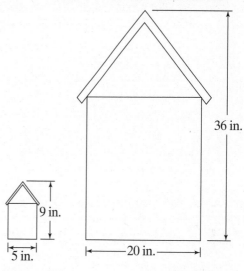

8. A map of the United States uses the scale 1 in. : 120 mi. On the map, Boston and Washington, D.C. are about 3.6 in. apart. What is the actual distance between these cities?

9. A 6-ft-tall man casts a shadow 20 ft long. At the same time of day, a nearby tree casts a shadow 50 ft long. What is the height of the tree?

10. Write $\frac{3}{8}$ as a decimal and as a percent.

11. Write 46% as a fraction in lowest terms.

12. Estimate 41% of 151.

13. What number is 30% of 180?

14. 42 is 5% of what number?

15. Last year Jonathan earned $6.00 per hour. This year he earns $7.25 per hour. Find the percent of increase. Round to the nearest percent.

16. William bought roses wholesale for $17.25 per dozen. He sold them for $25.00 per dozen. What was the percent markup?

17. How much will you pay for a CD priced at $12.99 if it is on sale for 15% off?

18. Find the retail cost of a coat if the wholesale cost is $90 and the markup is 58%.

19. What is the wholesale price if the retail markup is 25% and the retail price is $15.65?

20. Joshua deposited $250 into a savings account that pays 6% simple interest per year. How much interest will Joshua have earned after 3 years?

21. Suzanne invests $3,200 into an account that pays 4.3% simple interest. What is the final balance in the account after 6 years?

22. A bag contains 4 apples, 2 peaches, and 6 nectarines. Find the probability that a randomly selected piece of fruit is an apple.

23. Solve. $4x + 7 = 45$

24. Solve. $27 + \frac{g}{14} = 40$

25. Sam bought packs of baseball cards for $.79 each and a card container for $3.98. The total cost of Sam's purchases was $7.93. How many packs of cards did she buy?

Simplify.

26. $-7b + 24 + 10b - 8$

27. $-4(x + 7) + 5x$

Solve.

28. $17 + 3m = 2 + 8m$

29. $-12 - 7z = 16 + 5z$

30. $p + 4 > 16$

31. $x - 0.234 \geq 7.021$

32. Write an inequality for this graph.

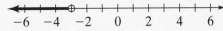

Solve.

33. $\frac{r}{14} > 1$

34. $-8w \leq 4$

35. $6 < \frac{s}{-8}$

Quarter 2 Test

Form B

Chapters 4–6

1. Find the unit rate for 123 words typed in 3 minutes.

2. Find an equal rate.
   30 gal/h = __?__ pt/min

3. Nina attends a school with a male-to-female ratio of 4 to 5 among students. If 192 students at this school are male, find the number of female students and the total number of students.

4. Solve. $\frac{5}{12} = \frac{60}{x}$

5. Are the rectangles similar? Explain.

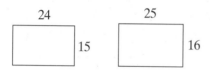

6. For the pair of similar polygons, find the missing side length *n*.

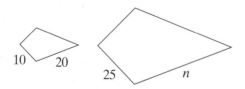

7. The car diagram below was enlarged. Find the scale factor.

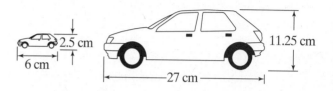

8. A map uses the scale 1 in. : 75 mi. On the map, two cities are about 3.6 in. apart. What is the actual distance between the cities?

9. A 10 ft. tall oak tree casts a shadow 50 ft. long. At the same time of day, a nearby building casts a shadow 90 ft. long. What is the height of the building?

10. Write $\frac{7}{50}$ as a decimal and as a percent.

11. Write 45% as a fraction in lowest terms.

12. Estimate 32% of 271.

13. What number is 40% of 260?

14. 26 is 2% of what number?

15. Last month Anna's allowance was $7.00 a week. This month it is $8.80 per week. Find the percent of increase.

16. Brad won a toaster worth $20. He preferred the one he had, so he sold the toaster at a garage sale for $8. What was the percent of discount?

17. How much will you pay for a DVD originally priced at $19.99 if it is on sale for 20% off?

18. Find the retail cost of a jacket if the wholesale cost is $50 and the markup is 75%.

19. What is the wholesale price of a bicycle if the retail markup is 40% and the retail price is $50?

20. Jenna took out a loan of $500 for 5 years. If she pays 8% simple interest, what is the interest she must pay at the end of 5 years?

21. Stan invests $5,500 into a savings account that pays 6.2% simple interest. What is the final balance in the account after 3 years?

22. A bowl contains 9 strawberries, 3 blueberries, and 4 blackberries. Find the probability that a randomly selected berry is a blackberry.

23. Solve. $e - 11 = 2.9$

24. Solve. $3x + 11 = -10$

25. Mrs. Baker purchased a number of juice boxes at a cost of $.30 each and a loaf of bread that cost $1.19. The total cost of her purchases was $2.99. Write an equation to determine how many juice boxes Mrs. Baker purchased.

Simplify.

26. $16m + 39 - 21m - 7$

27. $8x - 3(x + 11)$

Solve.

28. $18 + 3n = 7n + 6$

29. $-23 + 9t = -t - 3$

30. $y - 7 > 24$

31. $1.4 + x \leq 7$

32. Write the inequality for the graph.

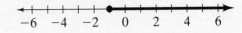

Solve.

33. $\frac{m}{10} < -4$

34. $\frac{s}{-13} > -4$

35. $-12x \leq -3$

Quarter 2 Test

Form D

Chapters 4–6

1. Find the unit pay rate of $26.50 for 5 hours of work.

2. Find an equal rate.
   44 ft/s = __?__ mi/h

3. Carol found she had a mystery-to-comedy videotape ratio of 8 to 3. If she has 36 comedy tapes in her collection, how many mystery tapes does she have? What is the total number of tapes?

4. Solve. $\frac{18}{q} = \frac{30}{65}$

5. Are the rectangles similar? Explain.

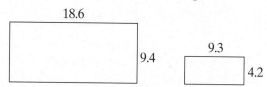

6. The two figures are similar. Find x.

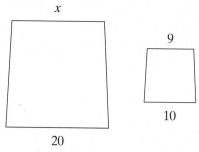

7. For a drawing that requires less detail, an architect has taken the drawing of a building and reduced it. Find the scale factor.

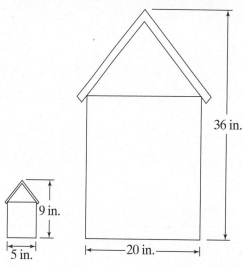

8. A map of the United States uses the scale 1 in. : 120 mi. On the map, Boston and Washington, D.C. are about 3.6 in. apart. What is the actual distance between these cities?

9. A 6-ft-tall man casts a shadow 20 ft long. At the same time of day, a nearby tree casts a shadow 50 ft long. What is the height of the tree?

10. Write $\frac{3}{8}$ as a decimal and as a percent.

11. Write 46% as a fraction in lowest terms.

12. Estimate 41% of 151.

13. What number is 30% of 180?

14. Last year Jonathan earned $6.00 per hour. This year he earns $7.25 per hour. Find the percent of increase. Round to the nearest percent.

15. How much will you pay for a CD priced at $12.99 if it is on sale for 15% off?

16. Find the retail cost of a coat if the wholesale cost is $90 and the markup is 58%.

17. Joshua deposited $250 into a savings account that pays 6% simple interest per year. How much interest will Joshua have earned after 3 years?

18. A bag contains 4 apples, 2 peaches, and 6 nectarines. Find the probability that a randomly selected piece of fruit is an apple.

19. Solve. $4x + 7 = 45$

20. Solve. $27 + \frac{g}{14} = 40$

21. Sam bought packs of baseball cards for $.79 each and a card container for $3.98. The total cost of Sam's purchases was $7.93. How many packs of cards did she buy?

Simplify.

22. $-4(x + 7) + 5x$

Solve.

23. $17 + 3m = 2 + 8m$

24. $p + 4 > 16$

25. Write an inequality for this graph.

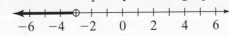

Solve.

26. $\frac{r}{14} > 1$

27. $-8w \le 4$

Quarter 2 Test

Form E

Chapters 4–6

1. Find the unit rate for 123 words typed in 3 minutes.

2. Find an equal rate.
   30 gal/h = __?__ pt/m

3. Nina attends a school with a male-to-female ratio of 4 to 5 among students. If 192 students at this school are male, find the number of female students and the total number of students.

4. Solve. $\frac{5}{12} = \frac{60}{x}$

5. Are the rectangles similar? Explain.

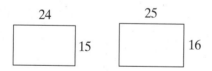

6. For the pair of similar polygons, find the missing side length n.

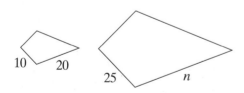

7. The car diagram below was enlarged. Find the scale factor.

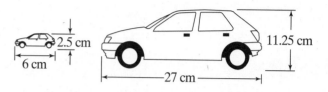

8. A map uses the scale 1 in. : 75 mi. On the map, two cities are about 3.6 in. apart. What is the actual distance between the cities?

9. A 10 ft. tall oak tree casts a shadow 50 ft. long. At the same time of day, a nearby building casts a shadow 90 ft. long. What is the height of the building?

10. Write $\frac{7}{50}$ as a decimal and as a percent.

11. Write 45% as a fraction in lowest terms.

12. Estimate 32% of 271.

13. What number is 40% of 260?

14. Brad won a toaster worth $20. He preferred the one he had, so he sold the toaster at a garage sale for $8. What was the percent of discount?

Simplify.

22. $8x - 3(x + 11)$

15. How much will you pay for a DVD originally priced at $19.99 if it is on sale for 20% off?

Solve.

23. $18 + 3n = 7n + 6$

16. Find the retail cost of a jacket if the wholesale cost is $50 and the markup is 75%.

24. $y - 7 > 24$

17. Jenna took out a loan of $500 for 5 years. If she pays 8% simple interest, what is the interest she must pay at the end of 5 years?

25. Write the inequality for the graph.

18. A bowl contains 9 strawberries, 3 blueberries, and 4 blackberries. Find the probability that a randomly selected berry is a blackberry.

Solve.

26. $\frac{m}{10} < -4$

19. Solve. $e - 11 = 2.9$

27. $\frac{s}{-13} > -4$

20. Solve. $3x + 11 = -10$

21. Mrs. Baker purchased a number of juice boxes at a cost of $.30 each and a loaf of bread that cost $1.19. The total cost of her purchases was $2.99. Write an equation to determine how many juice boxes Mrs. Baker purchased.

Quarter 3 Test

Form A

Chapters 7–9

1. Name an angle adjacent to ∠DFC.

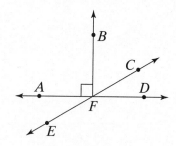

2. Use the diagram below to find the measures of ∠1, ∠2, and ∠3.

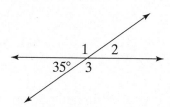

3. Find the measure of the complement of an angle with measure 47°.

4. Find the measure of the supplement of an angle with measure 128°.

5. Name the two pairs of alternate interior angles in the figure.

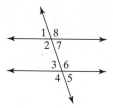

6. In the figure below, line *p* is parallel to line *m*. If *m*∠7 = 63°, find *m*∠4.

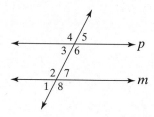

7. Determine whether the triangles are congruent. Explain.

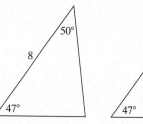

8. Draw and label a scalene obtuse triangle.

9. Determine the best name for the quadrilateral.

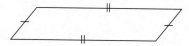

10. Find the measure of each angle of a regular hexagon.

11. Find the area.

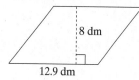

12. Find the circumference of the circle. Use 3.14 for π.

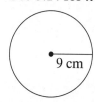

13. Find the area of the circle. Use 3.14 for π.

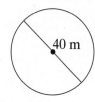

14. Construct an angle congruent to the angle below.

15. Draw $\overline{MN}$ with a length of 4 in. Construct the perpendicular bisector of $\overline{MN}$.

16. In the solid, identify a pair of skew lines.

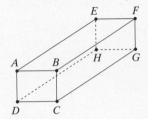

17. Draw a base plan of the three-dimensional object shown.

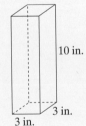

18. Draw the net of the object shown.

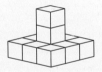

For Exercises 19 and 20, find the lateral area and the surface area of each figure. Use 3.14 for π.

19.

10 in.

3 in.
3 in.

20.

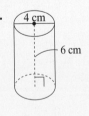

4 cm

6 cm

For Exercises 21 and 22, find the volume of each figure. Use 3.14 for π.

21.

6 m
9 m
16 m

22.

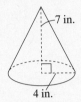

7 in.
4 in.

23. Find the volume of the rectangular prism if the dimensions are reduced by a ratio of $\frac{3}{4}$.

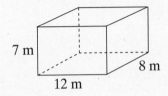

7 m
8 m
12 m

For Exercises 24 and 25, use the table below.

Name	Shots Made	Name	Shots Made
Teri	6	Esmeralda	5
Lupe	5	Connie	3
Tara	7	Keisha	4
Sally	2	April	1
Dawna	5	Tahsa	9

24. The ten girls who tried out for the basketball team each shot ten free throws. The table above show how many shots each girl made. Make a frequency table.

25. Display the results of the tryouts from Exercise 24 as a line plot.

26. Make a stem-and-leaf plot for these test scores: 83, 67, 91, 85, 88, 78, 85, 95, 89, 85, 82

Quarter 3 Test

Form B

Chapters 7–9

1. Name an angle adjacent to ∠*BFC*.

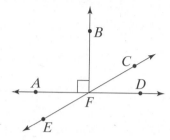

2. Use the diagram below to find the measures of ∠1, ∠2, and ∠3.

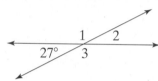

3. Find the measure of the complement of an angle with measure 56°.

4. Find the measure of the supplement of an angle with measure 107°.

5. In the figure, name the four pairs of corresponding angles.

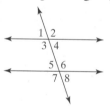

6. In the figure below, line *a* is parallel to line *b*. If *m*∠3 = 113°, find *m*∠4.

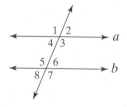

7. Determine whether the triangles are congruent. Explain.

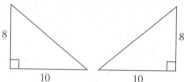

8. Draw and label an acute isosceles triangle.

9. Determine the best name for this quadrilateral.

10. Find the measure of each angle of a regular pentagon.

11. Find the area.

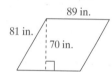

12. Find the circumference of the circle. Use 3.14 for *π*.

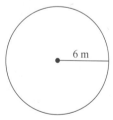

13. Find the area of the circle. Use 3.14 for *π*.

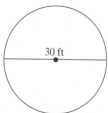

14. Construct ∠*MAT* congruent to ∠*RUG*.

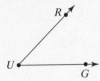

15. Draw $\overline{MN}$ with a length of 6 cm. Construct the perpendicular bisector of $\overline{MN}$.

16. In the solid, identify a pair of skew lines.

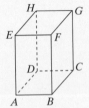

17. Draw a base plan of the 3-dimensional object shown.

18. Draw a net for the object shown.

For Exercises 19 and 20, find the lateral area and the surface area of each figure. Use 3.14 for π.

19.

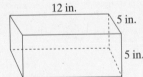

20.

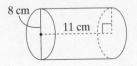

For Exercises 21 and 22, find the volume of each figure. Use 3.14 for π.

21.

22.

23. Find the volume of the rectangular prism if the dimensions are reduced by the ratio of $\frac{2}{5}$.

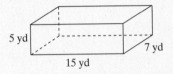

For Exercises 24 and 25, use the table below.

Name	Number of Shots	Name	Number of Shots
Tyler	3	Maria	1
Lyla	2	Luis	2
Terrell	4	Edward	2
Jin	4	Chandra	5
Davis	5	Kyle	4

24. Ten children are playing miniature golf at Tyler's birthday. The table above shows how many shots each child took to complete hole number 12. Make a frequency table.

25. Display the number of shots from Exercise 24 as a line plot.

26. Make a stem-and-leaf plot for these basketball scores:
78, 84, 99, 91, 85, 79, 83, 90, 101, 95

Quarter 3 Test

Chapters 7–9

Form D

1. Name an angle adjacent to $\angle DFC$.

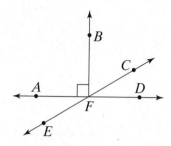

2. Use the diagram below to find the measures of $\angle 1$, $\angle 2$, and $\angle 3$.

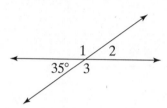

3. Find the measure of the complement of an angle with measure $47°$.

4. Find the measure of the supplement of an angle with measure $128°$.

5. Name the two pairs of alternate interior angles in the figure.

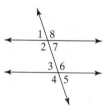

6. In the figure below, line p is parallel to line m. If $m\angle 7 = 63°$, find $m\angle 4$.

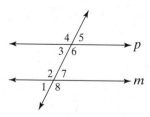

7. Determine whether the triangles are congruent. Explain.

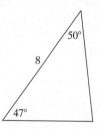 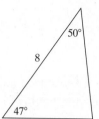

8. Determine the best name for the quadrilateral.

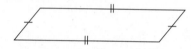

9. Find the measure of each angle of a regular hexagon.

10. Find the area.

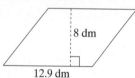

11. Find the circumference of the circle. Use 3.14 for π.

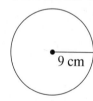

12. Find the area of the circle. Use 3.14 for π.

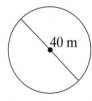

13. Construct an angle congruent to the angle below.

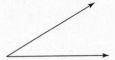

14. Draw $\overline{MN}$ with a length of 4 in. Construct the perpendicular bisector of $\overline{MN}$.

15. In the solid, identify a pair of skew lines.

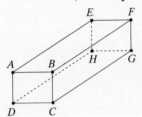

16. Draw a base plan of the three-dimensional object shown.

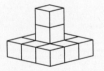

17. Draw the net of the object shown.

18. Find the lateral area and the surface area of the figure.

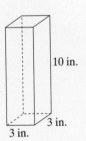

19. Find the volume of the figure.

For Exercises 20 and 21, use the table below.

Name	Shots Made	Name	Shots Made
Teri	6	Esmeralda	5
Lupe	5	Connie	3
Tara	7	Keisha	4
Sally	2	April	1
Dawna	5	Tahsa	9

20. The ten girls who tried out for the basketball team each shot ten free throws. The table above shows how many shots each girl made. Make a frequency table.

21. Display the results of the tryouts from Exercise 20 as a line plot

22. Make a stem-and-leaf plot for these test scores: 83, 67, 91, 85, 88, 78, 85, 95, 89, 85, 82

Quarter 3 Test

Form E

Chapters 7–9

1. Name an angle adjacent to ∠*BFC*.

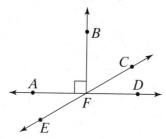

2. Use the diagram below to find the measures of ∠1, ∠2, and ∠3.

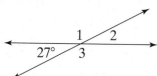

3. Find the measure of the complement of an angle with measure 56°.

4. Find the measure of the supplement of an angle with measure 107°.

5. In the figure, name the four pairs of corresponding angles.

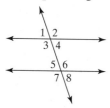

6. In the figure below, line *a* is parallel to line *b*. If *m*∠3 = 113°, find *m*∠4.

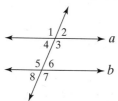

7. Determine whether the triangles are congruent. Explain.

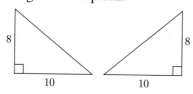

8. Determine the best name for this quadrilateral.

9. Find the measure of each angle of a regular pentagon.

10. Find the area.

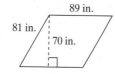

11. Find the circumference of the circle. Use 3.14 for π.

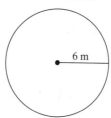

12. Find the area of the circle. Use 3.14 for π.

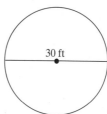

13. Construct ∠*MAT* congruent to ∠*RUG*.

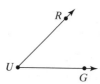

14. Draw $\overline{MN}$ with a length of 6 cm. Construct the perpendicular bisector of $\overline{MN}$.

15. In the solid, identify a pair of skew lines.

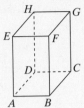

16. Draw a base plan of the 3-dimensional object shown.

17. Draw a net for the object shown.

18. Find the lateral area and the surface area of the figure.

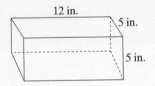

19. Find the volume of the figure.

For Exercises 20 and 21, use the table below.

Name	Number of Shots	Name	Number of Shots
Tyler	3	Maria	1
Lyla	2	Luis	2
Terrell	4	Edward	2
Jin	4	Chandra	5
Davis	5	Kyle	4

20. Ten children are playing miniature golf at Tyler's birthday. The table above shows how many shots each child took to complete hole number 12. Make a frequency table.

21. Display the number of shots from Exercise 20 as a plot line.

22. Make a stem-and-leaf plot for these basketball scores: 78, 84, 99, 91, 85, 79, 83, 90, 101, 95

Quarter 4 Test

Form A

Chapters 10–12

1. A number cube is rolled 360 times and the results are recorded as follows: 57 ones, 62 twos, 51 threes, 60 fours, 59 fives, and 71 sixes. What is the experimental probability of rolling an even number?

2. From a barrel of colored marbles, you randomly select 7 blue, 5 yellow, 8 red, 4 green, and 6 purple. Find the experimental probability of NOT selecting a purple marble.

3. Explain the differences between experimental and theoretical probability.

4. The probability that the city bus is running late is $\frac{1}{4}$. If the bus stops at your corner 12 times a day, predict how many times it will be on time.

5. At a small, local airport, Beverly asked 75 people eating in the cafeteria if they like to fly. Did Beverly take a random sample for her survey?

6. A drawer contains 2 red socks, 8 white socks, and 10 blue socks. Without looking, you draw out a sock, return it, and draw out a second sock. What is the probability that the first sock is blue and the second sock is white?

7. Ten runners compete in a 100-meter dash. Medals are awarded for first, second, and third place. How many different arrangements of three winners are possible?

8. The computer store has 9 service technicians. Three service technicians work each shift. How many different 3-technician groups can be formed?

9. Simplify. $_8C_5$

10. Find the first four terms of the sequence represented by the expression $2 - 8n$.

11. Find the common difference of the arithmetic sequence. $-1, 13, 27, 41, \ldots$

12. The graph below shows the growth of a particular plant over a period of 25 days. During which 5-day period did the plant grow the most?

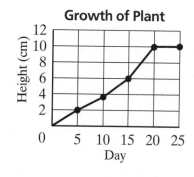

Growth of Plant

For Exercises 13 and 14, use the function rule $f(x) = -3x + 7$. **Find each value.**

13. $f(-2)$ **14.** $f(10)$

15. Cindy's car uses 0.04 gallons of gasoline for each mile she drives. Use function notation to show the total amount of gasoline used as a function of the number of miles Cindy drives.

16. What is the slope of the line on the graph below?

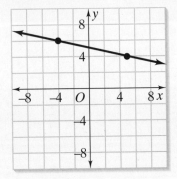

17. The table shows points on a line. Find the slope of the line.

x	1	2	3	4	5
y	−14	−19	−24	−29	−34

18. Graph the linear function $y = 3x - 2$.

19. Make a table and a graph for the quadratic function $f(x) = -3x^2 + 15$.

20. Simplify.

$-3b + 5 + 6a + a - b$

21. Find the sum.

$(3b^2 + 7b - 1) + (b^2 - 4b + 6)$

22. Find the difference.

$(2a^2 + 5a + 3) - (a^2 + 4a + 1)$

For Exercises 23–27, write each expression using a single exponent.

23. $y^8 \cdot y^5$ **24.** $2.6^{10} \cdot 2.6^3$

25. $\dfrac{x^5}{x^2}$ **26.** $(w^6)^{-2}$

27. $(5x^3)^2$

28. Light travels at 3.00×10^8 m/s. How many seconds does a light ray take to travel 12×10^9 m?

29. Multiply. $3u^2(2u^4 + u^3 - 2u)$

30. Simplify. $(4b)^0$

Quarter 4 Test

Form B

Chapters 10–12

1. A number cube is rolled 360 times and the results are recorded as follows: 57 ones, 62 twos, 51 threes, 60 fours, 59 fives, and 71 sixes. What is the experimental probability of rolling an odd number?

2. From a barrel of colored marbles, you randomly select 7 blue, 5 yellow, 8 red, 4 green, and 6 purple. Find the experimental probability of NOT selecting a blue marble.

3. Explain the differences between dependent and independent events.

4. The probability that the city bus is running late is $\frac{1}{3}$. If the bus stops at your corner 15 times a day, predict how many times it will be on time.

5. At a mall, Terry asked shoppers what kind of pet (or pets) they own. Did Terry take a random sample for his survey?

6. Two jars each contain red balls and green balls. Jar I contains 2 red balls and 6 green balls. Jar II contains 5 red balls and 4 green balls. A ball is drawn at random from each jar. What is the probability that both balls are green?

7. The video store has 9 "high-seas-adventure" movies. How many ways can you arrange an "all-day show" of 4 of them?

8. The computer store offers 12 different kinds of "good-deal" coupons. How many different ways can you select 4 of the coupons?

9. Simplify. $_7P_3$

10. Find the first four terms of the sequence represented by the expression $5 - 6n$.

11. Find the common ratio of the geometric sequence. $-\frac{3}{4}, \frac{3}{8}, -\frac{3}{16}, \ldots$

12. The graph below shows the growth of a particular plant over a period of 25 days. During which 5-day period did the plant grow the least?

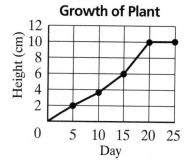

Growth of Plant

For Exercises 13 and 14, use the function rule $f(x) = -3x + 7$. **Find each value.**

13. $f(-4)$ 14. $f(7)$

15. A small aircraft uses 6 gallons of gasoline for each mile it travels. Use function notation to show the total amount of gasoline used as a function of the number of miles traveled.

16. What is the slope of the line on the graph below?

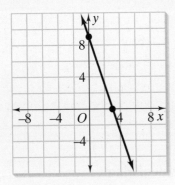

17. The table shows points on a line. Find the slope of the line.

x	1	2	3	4	5
y	5	9	13	17	21

18. Graph the linear function $y = 4x + 1$.

19. Make a table and a graph for the quadratic function $f(x) = 4x^2 - 8$.

20. Simplify.

$$-8k + 50 + 2m + 4m - k$$

21. Find the sum.

$$(2a^3 - 7a^2 + 5) + (a^3 + 4a^2 - 2a)$$

22. Find the difference.

$$(4q^2 + 3q + 9) - (3q^2 - 2q + 7)$$

For Exercises 23–27, write each expression using a single exponent.

23. $x^5 \cdot x^7$ 24. $1.4^{10} \cdot 1.4^6$

25. $\dfrac{m^7}{m^5}$ 26. $(k^5)^{-2}$

27. $(4b^6)^2$

28. Light travels at 3.00×10^8 m/s. How many seconds does a light ray take to travel 15×10^9 m?

29. Multiply. $2v^3(7v^3 - 8v^2 + 4v)$

30. Simplify. $(4b)^{-1}$

Quarter 4 Test

Form D

Chapters 10–12

1. From a barrel of colored marbles, you randomly select 7 blue, 5 yellow, 8 red, 4 green, and 6 purple. Find the experimental probability of NOT selecting a purple marble.

2. Explain the differences between experimental and theoretical probability.

3. The probability that the city bus is running late is $\frac{1}{4}$. If the bus stops at your corner 12 times a day, predict how many times it will be on time.

4. At a small, local airport, Beverly asked 75 people eating in the cafeteria if they like to fly. Did Beverly take a random sample for her survey?

5. A drawer contains 2 red socks, 8 white socks, and 10 blue socks. Without looking, you draw out a sock, return it, and draw out a second sock. What is the probability that the first sock is blue and the second sock is white?

6. Ten runners compete in a 100-meter dash. Medals are awarded for first, second, and third place. How many different arrangements of three winners are possible?

7. The computer store has 9 service technicians. Three service technicians work each shift. How many different 3-technician groups can be formed?

8. Simplify. $_8C_5$

9. Find the first four terms of the sequence represented by the expression $2 - 8n$.

10. Find the common difference of the arithmetic sequence. $-1, 13, 27, 41, \ldots$

11. The graph below shows the growth of a particular plant over a period of 25 days. During which 5-day period did the plant grow the most?

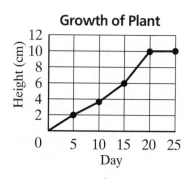

12. Use the function rule $f(x) = -3x + 7$. Find $f(10)$.

13. Cindy's car uses .04 gallons of gasoline for each mile she drives. Use function notation to show the total amount of gasoline used as a function of the number of miles Cindy drives.

14. What is the slope of the line on the graph below?

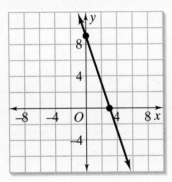

15. Graph the linear function $y = 3x - 2$.

16. Make a table and a graph for the quadratic function $f(x) = -3x^2 - 15$.

17. Find the sum.

    $(3b^2 + 7b - 1) + (b^2 - 4b + 6)$

18. Find the difference.

    $(2a^2 + 5a + 3) - (a^2 + 4a + 1)$

19. Write $y^8 \cdot y^5$ using a single exponent.

20. Multiply. $3u^2(2u^4 + u^3 - 2u)$

21. Write $\frac{x^5}{x^2}$ using a single exponent.

22. Simplify. $(4b)^0$

23. Write $(5x^3)^2$ using a single exponent.

Quarter 4 Test

Chapters 10–12

Form E

1. From a barrel of colored marbles, you randomly select 7 blue, 5 yellow, 4 green, 8 red, and 6 purple. Find the experimental probability of NOT selecting a blue marble.

2. Explain the differences between dependent and independent events.

3. The probability that the city bus is running late is $\frac{1}{3}$. If the bus stops at your corner 15 times a day, predict how many times it will be on time.

4. At a mall, Terry asked shoppers what kind of pet (or pets) they own. Did Terry take a random sample for his survey?

5. Two jars each contain red balls and green balls. Jar I contains 2 red balls and 6 green balls. Jar II contains 5 red balls and 4 green balls. A ball is drawn at random from each jar. What is the probability that both balls are green?

6. The video store has 9 "high-seas-adventure" movies. How many ways can you arrange an "all-day show" of 4 of them?

7. The computer store offers 12 different kinds of "good-deal" coupons. How many different ways can you select 4 of the coupons?

8. Simplify. $_7P_3$

9. Find the first four terms of the sequence represented by the expression $5 - 6n$.

10. Find the common ratio of the geometric sequence. $-\frac{3}{4}, \frac{3}{8}, -\frac{3}{16}, \cdots$

11. The graph below shows the growth of a particular plant over a period of 25 days. During which 5-day period did the plant grow the least?

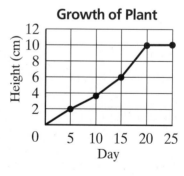

Growth of Plant

12. Use the function rule $f(x) = -3x + 7$.
Find $f(7)$.

13. A small aircraft uses 6 gallons of gasoline for each mile it travels. Use function notation to show the total amount of gasoline used as a function of the number of miles traveled.

14. What is the slope of the line on the graph below?

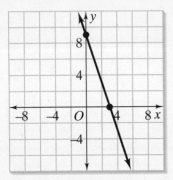

15. Graph the linear function $y = 4x + 1$.

16. Make a table and a graph for the quadratic function $f(x) = 4x^2 - 8$.

17. Find the sum.

$$(2a^3 - 7a^2 + 5) + (a^3 + 4a^2 - 2a)$$

18. Find the difference.

$$(4q^2 + 3q + 9) - (3q^2 - 2q + 7)$$

19. Write $x^5 \cdot x^7$ using a single exponent.

20. Multiply. $2v^3(7v^3 - 8v^2 + 4v)$

21. Write $\frac{m^7}{m^5}$ using a single exponent.

22. Simplify. $(4b)^{-1}$

23. Write $(4b^6)^2$ using a single exponent.

Mid-Course Test
Chapters 1–6

Form A

1. Evaluate the expression $3x(5 + y)$ for $x = 7$ and $y = -2$.

2. Simplify. $(-15) \cdot (-5) + 84 \div (-4)$

3. Add. $5 + 7 + (-5) + (-4)$

4. Use the Distributive Property to rewrite $3(2 + 5)$.

5. Write an expression for 10 less than twice a number n.

6. Simplify. $-4 + 2 \cdot 5^2$

7. Simplify. $|-9| - 3$

8. Solve and graph the solution.
   $7x - 3 \leq 11$

9. Solve. $25x - 5 = 145$

10. Solve. $\frac{1}{5}x + 1 = 13$

11. What values of x are solutions described by this graph?

12. Wilma has a part-time job that pays $5 per hour. How many hours must she work in a week to earn at least $40? Write and solve an inequality.

13. Simplify. $5(2x - 7) + 11$

14. Solve. $-3(t - 4) + 5t = 5(8 - t)$

15. Write 3,480,000 in scientific notation.

16. Write 4.5×10^{-6} in standard form.

17. Find the coordinates of points A and B.

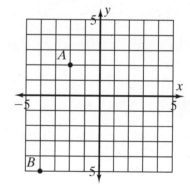

18. Which of the following is *not* a solution of $y = x + 5$?
(3, 8), (5, 12), (0, 5), (1, 6)

19. In which quadrant is the point with coordinates (8, 4)?

20. $\triangle ABC$ has vertices $A(1, -2)$, $B(2, 1)$, and $C(2, -2)$. Graph $\triangle ABC$ and its image after a counter-clockwise rotation of 90° about the origin.

21. Solve. $\frac{x}{-6} \geq -8$

22. Graph the equation. $y = -2x + 1$

23. A baseball bat and 3 baseballs cost $159.99. The bat costs $132.00. How much does one baseball cost? Write and solve an equation to answer the question.

24. 52 people will attend a banquet. 8 people can sit at each table. How many tables are needed? Write and solve an inequality to answer the question.

25. How many lines of symmetry does this figure have?

26. If $\triangle ABC$ is reflected over the *x*-axis to produce $\triangle A'B'C'$, give the coordinates of A'.

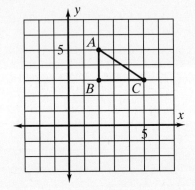

27. Order the numbers from least to greatest.
$-\frac{3}{4}, -1.2, \frac{5}{6}, \frac{2}{3}$

28. Find the prime factorization of 425.

29. Find the two square roots of 81.

Mid-Course Test (continued)   Form A

Chapters 1–6

For Exercises 30-32, simplify each expression. Write the answer as a fraction or mixed number in simplest form.

30. $3\frac{1}{2} \cdot 2\frac{1}{3}$

31. $4\frac{1}{5} - 2\frac{5}{6}$

32. $5\frac{5}{6} \div 1\frac{3}{4}$

33. Determine whether the side lengths 5, 12, and 13 could form a right triangle. Explain your answer.

34. Solve for w.
$V = lwh$

35. Find the GCF of 40 and 64.

36. Find the missing length.

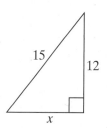

37. Write $\frac{88}{132}$ as a fraction in simplest form.

38. What would be an appropriate metric unit to measure the distance from Earth to the Sun?

39. Coree can type 4,591 words in one hour. The requirement to pass her typing class is 75 words per minute. Determine whether Coree has met her requirement.

40. Triangle DEF has vertices $(0, 0)$, $(0, -6)$, and $(-3, -9)$. What would be the vertices of $D'E'F'$ if the scale factor is $\frac{2}{3}$ and the center is the origin?

41. Barbara bought 3.5 lb of mixed nuts for $22.75. How much was the cost per pound of the mixed nuts?

42. Rachel made 12 sandwiches in 15 minutes. At that rate, how long would it take her to make 20 sandwiches?

43. Solve the proportion. $\frac{18}{q} = \frac{30}{65}$

44. The actual length of a puma is 2.45 m. The scale of a drawing of a puma is 1 cm : 0.5 m. Find the length of the puma in the drawing, to the nearest tenth of a centimeter.

45. Sue charges $2.25 per hour for the first 3 hours she baby-sits and $1.75 for each additional hour. Write an expression to determine how much Sue charges to baby-sit four hours or longer.

46. Paula sold 35 packages of wrapping paper for the Booster Club fund-raiser. This is one less than twice the number of packages that she sold last year. How many packages did Paula sell last year?

47. Find the length of $\overline{MN}$.

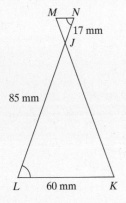

48. Write $1\frac{4}{5}$ as a percent.

49. Estimate. 61% of 42

50. 18 is 60% of what number?

51. Write an equation to solve the problem. What is 77% of 48?

52. What is the sale price of a $24.99 book marked 10% off?

53. What is the final price of a sweatshirt that sells for $15.99, if the tax is 7.25%?

54. A department store purchases a dress for $60. To sell the dress to customers, the price is marked up by 21%. What is the new price of the dress?

55. Find the simple interest paid on a loan of $500 at 12% for 3 years.

56. Cody's family borrowed $4,000 for 2 years at 15% interest compounded annually. How much will they owe?

Mid-Course Test   Form B

Chapters 1–6

1. Evaluate $5p + 3q$ when $p = -2$ and $q = 3$.

2. Simplify. $-3 + (7 + 5) \div (-3)$

3. Subtract. $61 - (-18) - 5$

4. Rewrite $-3(4 + 2)$ using the Distributive Property.

5. Write an algebraic expression for 9 times the sum of a number and 12.

6. Simplify. $20 - 4^2 + 12$

7. Find the sum. $-22 + |3|$

8. Solve and graph the solution. $5n + 23 > 3$

9. Solve. $6x - 4 = 20$

10. Solve. $\frac{p}{3} - 5 = 15$

11. What values of x are solutions described by this graph?

12. A machine can produce electric connectors at a rate of 25 per minute. How many minutes will it take the machine to produce at least 800 connectors? Write and solve an inequality.

13. Simplify. $3(7x - 8) + 16$

14. Solve. $2(t - 3) - 7t = 5(t + 2) + 4$

15. Write 5,489,000 in scientific notation.

16. Write 5.3×10^{-4} in standard form.

17. Find the coordinates of points *A* and *B*.

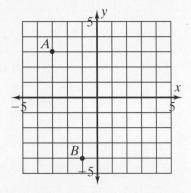

18. Which point is *not* on the graph of the equation $y = -3x + 1$?
$(1, 0), (3, -8), (0, 1), (2, -5)$

19. In what quadrant is the point $(-2, -5)$ located?

20. $\triangle DEF$ has vertices $D(1, 1)$, $E(2,4)$, and $F(3,1)$. Graph $\triangle DEF$ and its image after a counter-clockwise rotation of 90° about the origin.

21. Solve. $-4f \geq -64$

22. Graph the equation. $y = 4x - 2$

23. Jan bought a $34.00 pair of jeans and 3 shirts. Her total bill was $97.00. How much was each shirt? Write and solve an equation to answer the question.

24. How many lines of symmetry does this figure have?

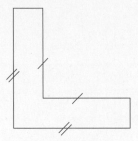

25. If $\triangle XYZ$ is reflected over the *y*-axis to produce $\triangle X'Y'Z'$, give the coordinates of X'.

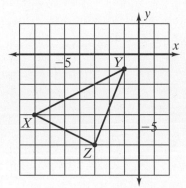

26. Order the numbers from greatest to least.
$5.16, 5\frac{1}{6}, 5.2, 5\frac{1}{8}$

27. Find the prime factorization of 890.

28. Find the two square roots of 121.

Mid-Course Test (continued)   Form B

Chapters 1–6

For Exercises 29–31, simplify each expression. Write the answer as a fraction or mixed number in simplest form.

29. $5\frac{1}{6} - 2\frac{7}{8}$

30. $2\frac{2}{3} \times 1\frac{1}{2}$

31. $1\frac{3}{4} \div 2\frac{1}{3}$

32. Determine whether the side lengths 5, 13, and 17 could make a right triangle. Explain your answer.

33. Solve for h.
$V = lwh$

34. Find the GCF of 24 and 120.

35. Find the missing length.

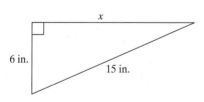

36. Write $\frac{56}{120}$ as a fraction in simplest form.

37. Which metric unit is best for measuring the length of a driveway?

38. Determine the number of ounces a 6.2 quart container can hold.

39. Given triangle RST with vertices $R(0,0)$, $S(0,-3)$, $T(-3,-6)$, give the coordinates of the vertices of $R'S'T'$, a dilation with scale factor $\frac{3}{2}$ and center at the origin.

40. At a garage sale, a box of 78 cookie cutters costs $19.50. What was the cost per cookie cutter?

41. Ed put together 10 display cases in 3 hours. About how many display cases can he put together in 40 hours?

42. Solve the proportion. $\frac{b}{92} = \frac{55}{115}$

43. A scale model of a redwood forest has a ratio of 1 in. : 40 ft. If the average tree is 220 feet tall, how tall would a tree on the scale model be?

44. Sue charges $3.50 per hour for the first 3 hours she baby-sits and $2.25 for each additional hour. Write an expression to determine how much Sue charges to baby-sit four hours or longer.

45. Paula sold 40 packages of wrapping paper for the Booster Club fund-raiser. This is four less than twice the number of packages that she sold last year. How many packages did Paula sell last year?

46. Find the length of $\overline{DE}$.

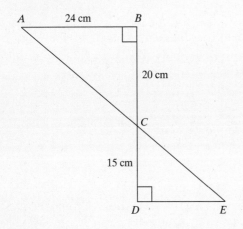

47. Write 2.6 as a percent.

48. Estimate. 21% of 12

49. 28 is 25% of what number?

50. Write an equation to solve the problem. 52 is 41% of what number?

51. The original price of a suit is $250. Find the sale price after it is marked down 20%.

52. Dennis bought two lamps for $80.00. If he was charged an additional 6% sales tax, what was his total payment?

53. The owner of a music store received a shipment of stereos at a cost of $160.00 each. What will the selling price be if he applies a 45% markup?

54. Find the simple interest on $900 invested at 8.5% for 3 years.

55. Find the final balance to the nearest cent on $1,100 compounded annually for 4 years at 7%.

56. 52 people will attend a banquet. 8 people can sit at each table. How many tables are needed? Write and solve an inequality to answer the question.

Mid-Course Test

Form D

Chapters 1–6

1. Evaluate the expression $3x(5 + y)$ for $x = 7$ and $y = -2$.

2. Simplify. $(-15) \cdot (-5) + 84 \div (-4)$

3. Add. $5 + 7 + (-5) + (-4)$

4. Use the Distributive Property to rewrite $3(2 + 5)$.

5. Write an expression for 10 less than twice a number n.

6. Simplify. $-4 + 2 \cdot 5^2$

7. Simplify. $|-9| - 3$

8. Solve and graph the solution.
$7x - 3 \le 11$

9. Solve. $25x - 5 = 145$

10. Solve. $\frac{1}{5}x + 1 = 13$

11. Wilma has a part-time job that pays $5 per hour. How many hours must she work in a week to earn at least $40? Write and solve an inequality.

12. Simplify. $5(2x - 7) + 11$

13. Solve. $-3(t - 4) + 5t = 5(8 - t)$

14. Write 3,480,000 in scientific notation.

15. Find the coordinates of points A and B.

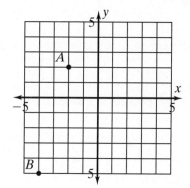

16. Which of the following is *not* a solution of $y = x + 5$?
$(3, 8), (5, 12), (0, 5), (1, 6)$

17. In which quadrant is the point with coordinates $(8, 4)$?

18. $\triangle ABC$ has vertices $A(1, -2)$, $B(2, 1)$, and $C(2, -2)$. Graph $\triangle ABC$ and its image after a counter-clockwise rotation of 90° about the origin.

19. Solve. $\frac{x}{-6} \geq -8$

20. Graph the equation. $y = -2x + 1$

21. You buy a notebook for $8.00 and 3 packages of writing paper. Your total is $12.50. How much does each package of writing paper cost? Write and solve an equation to answer the question.

22. How many lines of symmetry does this figure have?

23. If $\triangle ABC$ is reflected across the *x*-axis to produce $\triangle A'B'C'$, give the coordinates of A'.

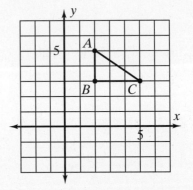

24. Order the numbers from least to greatest.
$-\frac{17}{20}, -0.8, \frac{3}{4}, \frac{13}{20}$

25. Find the prime factorization of 300.

26. Find the two square roots of 81.

Mid-Course Test (continued)

Chapters 1–6

For Exercises 27–29, simplify each expression. Write the answer as a fraction or mixed number in simplest form.

27. $3\frac{1}{2} \cdot 2\frac{1}{3}$

28. $5\frac{1}{4} - 2\frac{5}{6}$

29. $5\frac{5}{6} \div 1\frac{3}{4}$

30. Determine whether the side lengths 5, 12, and 13 could form a right triangle. Explain your answer.

31. Solve for w.
$V = lwh$

32. Find the GCF of 40 and 64.

33. Write $\frac{64}{96}$ as a fraction in simplest form.

34. What would be an appropriate metric unit to measure the distance from Earth to the Sun?

35. Coree can type 4,591 words in one hour. The requirement to pass her typing class is 75 words per minute. Determine whether Coree has met her requirement.

36. Triangle *DEF* has vertices $(0, 0)$, $(0, -6)$, and $(-3, -9)$. What would be the vertices of $D'E'F'$ if the scale factor is $\frac{2}{3}$ and the center is the origin?

37. Barbara bought 3.5 lb of mixed nuts for $10.50. How much was the cost per pound of the mixed nuts?

38. Rachel made 12 sandwiches in 15 minutes. At that rate, how long would it take her to make 20 sandwiches?

39. Solve the proportion. $\frac{9}{x} = \frac{3}{9}$

40. The actual length of a puma is 2.45 m. The scale of a drawing of a puma is 1 cm : 0.5 m. Find the length of the puma in the drawing, to the nearest tenth of a centimeter.

41. Sue charges $2.25 per hour for the first 3 hours she baby-sits and $1.75 for each additional hour. Write an expression to determine how much Sue charges to baby-sit four hours or longer.

42. Paula sold 35 packages of wrapping paper for the Booster Club fund-raiser. This is one less than twice the number of packages that she sold last year. How many packages did Paula sell last year?

43. Find the length of $\overline{MN}$.

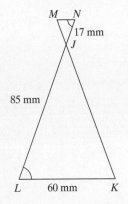

44. Write $1\frac{4}{5}$ as a percent.

45. Estimate. 61% of 42

46. 18 is 60% of what number?

47. Write an equation to solve the problem. What is 70% of 48?

48. What is the sale price of a $24.99 book marked 10% off?

49. What is the final price of a sweatshirt that sells for $15.99, if the tax is 7.25%?

50. Find the simple interest paid on a loan of $500 at 12% for 3 years.

51. Cody's family borrowed $4,000 for 2 years at 15% interest compounded annually. How much will they owe?

Mid-Course Test

Form E

Chapters 1–6

1. Evaluate $5p + 3q$ when $p = -2$ and $q = 3$.

2. Simplify. $-3 + (7 + 5) \div (-3)$

3. Subtract. $61 - (-18) - 5$

4. Rewrite $-3(4 + 2)$ using the Distributive Property.

5. Write an algebraic expression for 9 times the sum of a number and 12.

6. Simplify. $20 - 4^2 + 12$

7. Find the sum. $-22 + |3|$

8. Solve and graph the solution.
   $5n + 23 > 3$

9. Solve. $6x - 4 = 20$

10. Solve. $\frac{p}{3} - 5 = 15$

11. A machine can produce electric connectors at a rate of 25 per minute. How many minutes will it take the machine to produce at least 800 connectors? Write and solve an inequality.

12. Simplify. $3(7x - 8) + 16$

13. Solve. $2(t - 3) - 7t = 5(t + 2) + 4$

14. Write 5,489,000 in scientific notation.

Mid-Course Test (continued)   Form E

15. Find the coordinates of points *A* and *B*.

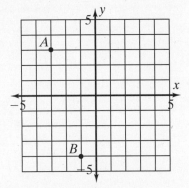

16. Which point is *not* on the graph of the equation $y = -3x + 1$?
$(1, 0), (3, -8), (0, 1), (2, -5)$

17. In what quadrant is the point $(-2, -5)$ located?

18. $\triangle DEF$ has vertices $D(1, 1)$, $E(2, 4)$, and $F(3, 1)$. Graph $\triangle DEF$ and its image after a counter-clockwise rotation of 90° about the origin.

19. Solve. $-4f \geq -64$

20. Graph the equation. $y = 4x - 2$

21. How many lines of symmetry does this figure have?

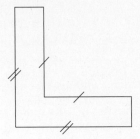

22. If $\triangle XYZ$ is reflected across the *y*-axis to produce $\triangle X'Y'Z'$, give the coordinates of X'.

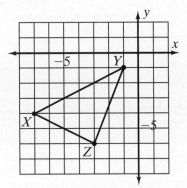

23. Order the numbers from greatest to least.
$-0.62, -\frac{5}{7}, \frac{2}{9}, \frac{1}{7}$

24. Find the prime factorization of 390.

25. Find the two square roots of 121.

Mid-Course Test (continued)

Chapters 1–6

For Exercises 26–28, simplify each expression. Write the answer as a fraction or mixed number in simplest form.

26. $5\frac{1}{6} - 2\frac{4}{5}$

27. $2\frac{2}{3} \times 1\frac{1}{2}$

28. $1\frac{3}{4} \div 2\frac{1}{3}$

29. Determine whether the side lengths 5, 13, and 17 could make a right triangle. Explain your answer.

30. Solve for h.
$V = lwh$

31. Find the GCF of 24 and 120.

32. Write $\frac{28}{60}$ as a fraction in simplest form.

33. Which metric unit is best for measuring the length of a driveway?

34. Determine the number of ounces a 6.2 quart container can hold.

35. Given triangle RST with vertices $R(0, 0)$, $S(0, -3)$, $T(-3, -6)$, give the coordinates of $R'S'T'$, a dilation with scale factor $\frac{3}{2}$ and center at the origin.

36. At a garage sale, a box of 78 cookie cutters costs $19.50. What was the cost per cookie cutter?

37. Ed put together 10 display cases in 3 hours. About how many display cases can he put together in 40 hours?

38. Solve the proportion. $\frac{19}{x} = \frac{38}{90}$

39. A scale model of a redwood forest has a ratio of 1 in. : 40 ft. If the average tree is 220 feet tall, how tall would a tree on the scale model be?

40. Sue charges $3.50 per hour for the first 3 hours she baby-sits and $2.25 for each additional hour. Write an expression to determine how much Sue charges to baby-sit four hours or longer.

41. Paula sold 40 packages of wrapping paper for the Booster Club fund-raiser. This is four less than twice the number of packages that she sold last year. How many packages did Paula sell last year?

42. Find the length of $\overline{DE}$.

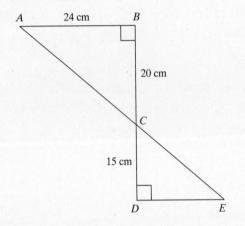

43. Write 2.6 as a percent.

44. Estimate. 21% of 12

45. 28 is 25% of what number?

46. Write an equation to solve the problem. 52 is 40% of what number?

47. The original price of a suit is $250. Find the sale price after it is marked down 20%.

48. Dennis bought two lamps for $80.00. If he was charged an additional 6% sales tax, what was his total payment?

49. Find the simple interest on $900 invested at 8.5% for 3 years.

50. Find the final balance to the nearest cent on $1,100 compounded annually for 4 years at 7%.

51. Jan bought a $34.00 pair of jeans and 3 shirts. Her total bill was $97.00. How much was each shirt? Write and solve an equation to answer the question.

Final Test

Form A

Chapters 1–12

1. Evaluate the expression $x(4 + 5y)$ for $x = 3$ and $y = 2.4$.

2. Simplify. $\dfrac{2 + 3(8 - 2)}{(-2)(-3) - 8}$

3. What is the median of this data set?
   $16, 13, 11, 16, 10, 17, 15$

4. Order from least to greatest.
   $-19, 0, 17, 20, -21$

5. Simplify. $(-25) - (-7) - 7$

6. Brad paid for two pounds of bananas with a $20 bill. He got back $18.60. What was the cost of one pound of bananas?

7. Solve. $z - 3 \geq 12$

8. A scoop of ice cream is $1.50. Each topping costs $.15. Write an algebraic expression representing the cost of a scoop of ice cream with x toppings.

9. Solve. $12w - 11 = 25$

10. Simplify. $9(x - 1) - 2(x - 1)$

11. Which ordered pair is a solution of the equation $5x + 3y = 13$?
    $(5, -4), (5, -3), (-3, 5), (-4, 5)$

12. A triangle has vertex coordinates $X(0, 0)$, $Y(2, 3)$, and $Z(-1, 4)$. Find the coordinates of X', Y', and Z' after a rotation of $180°$ about the origin.

13. Translate the triangle below 5 units to the left and 1 unit up. What are the coordinates of the image of the translation?

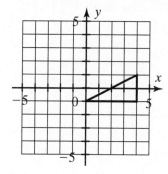

14. Identify $\sqrt{48}$ as rational or irrational. Explain your answer.

15. Find the length of the missing side of the triangle. Round to the nearest tenth if necessary.

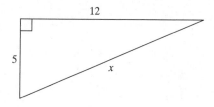

16. Brent has a board $2\frac{11}{12}$ feet long. He needs a board $3\frac{1}{6}$ feet long. How much longer does Brent's board need to be?

17. Write 0.45 as a fraction in simplest form.

18. Solve. $N + \frac{1}{3} = \frac{4}{5}$

19. Paul earned $63 in 3 hours. Find the hourly rate.

20. A flower shop sells 12 roses for $18.00. How much do they charge for 18 roses?

21. A tree casts a shadow of 100 feet, while a 5-foot person casts a shadow of 20 feet. Explain how you can use similar triangles to find the height of the tree. Then find the height of the tree.

22. Find the interest earned in a $900 savings account at a simple interest rate of $7\frac{1}{2}$% for 12 years.

23. 18,000 g = _?_ kg

24. Solve the proportion. $\frac{12}{30} = \frac{18}{m}$

25. Write the equation you would use to solve the problem. Then solve the problem. What is 26% of 59?

26. What is the sale price of a $93 item being discounted by 30%?

27. Estimate. 30% of 507

28. What is the final price of a $149 microwave oven with a markup of 12%?

29. Computer Depot buys a certain computer for $2,000 and sells it for $2,750. What is the percent of markup?

30. Find the product and write the answer in scientific notation.
$(2.3 \times 10^3) \cdot (4.1 \times 10^2)$

31. The approximate diameter of a cowpox virus is written as 2.5×10^{-7} m in scientific notation. How should this number be written in standard notation?

32. Write $\dfrac{(-6)^{11}}{(-6)^0}$ with one base and one exponent.

33. Simplify the expression. $(3p^0q^4)^3$

34. Explain why the triangles are congruent.

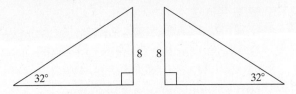

35. Find the area of the figure below.

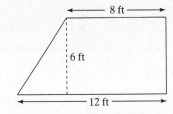

36. Line c is parallel to line d. Name the interior angles below.

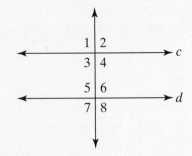

37. What is the measure of the supplement of an angle with a measure of 41°?

Final Test (continued)
Chapters 1–12

Form A

38. What is the sum of the measures of all angles in a hexagon?

39. Find the surface area of the prism.

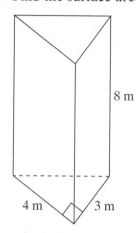

8 m

4 m   3 m

40. Find the volume of the cylindrical water bottle. Use 3.14 for π.

9 mm

35 mm

41. Find the volume of the cone. Use 3.14 for π.

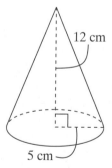

12 cm

5 cm

42. Identify the solid formed by this net.

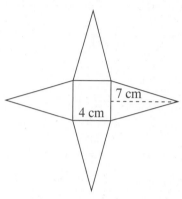

7 cm

4 cm

43. Find the volume of the rectangular prism after a dilation by a scale factor of 2.

1.2 in.

11 in.

0.4 in.

44. Name a type of data-display graph that displays data using equal intervals.

45. Identify the median in the data below.

Stem	Leaf
14	0 1 5 8
15	0 3 7
16	2 3 4 4 6 8
17	1 2 7 9

46. What is the upper quartile of the data in this box-and-whisker plot?

Scores on a
Social Studies Test

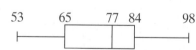

53   65   77   84   98

47. A scatterplot compared test grades and study time. What type of trend would you expect?

48. The circle graph shows data on the suitability of land for farming. What percentage of the land is too wet or too shallow?

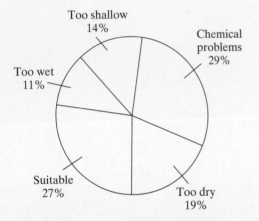

Too shallow
14%

Chemical problems
29%

Too wet
11%

Suitable
27%

Too dry
19%

49. Ms. Wong is redecorating her office. She has a choice of 3 colors of paint, 4 kinds of curtains, and 4 colors of carpet. How many different ways are there to redecorate?

50. How many ways can a president and vice-president be chosen from the 12-member math team?

51. A box contains 3 red pencils and 2 blue pencils. Two pencils are taken at random from the box in succession, without replacement. If the first pencil is red, what is the probability that the second pencil is red?

52. From a barrel of colored marbles, you randomly select 7 blue, 5 yellow, 8 red, 4 green, and 6 purple. Find the experimental probability of randomly selecting a marble that is NOT green.

53. You want to conduct a survey to find out how taxi drivers are affected by road construction. How can you survey a random sample?

54. Use the function rule $f(x) = 5x - 8$ to find $f(-3)$.

55. A sequence has a common ratio of $\frac{2}{3}$ and first term of 162. Find the next three terms.

56. Add. $\quad 2q^3 - q + 3$
$\underline{+ \qquad 7q + 9}$

57. Subtract. $\quad (3v^3 + 2v^2 - v + 1)$
$\underline{- (2v^3 + 2v^2 - 3v - 8)}$

58. Write the rule that relates x and y in the table.

x	1	2	3	4	5
y	3	6	9	12	15

Final Test

Form B

Chapters 1–12

1. Evaluate the expression $x(22 - 5y)$ for $x = 3$ and $y = 2.2$.

2. Simplify. $72 \div 8 - 1 + 6 \cdot 2 - 20$

3. Find the median for the ages of a group of friends.
   33 34 59 49 43 29 40 59

4. Order from least to greatest.
   $-5, -101, 88, 36, -77$

5. Subtract. $200 - (-100) - 59 - (-6) - 1$

6. A parking garage charges $2.50 to get in and $1.00 for each hour. If Al paid $8.50, for how long was his car parked in the garage?

7. Solve. $p + 3 \le 24$

8. Gretchen boxes widgets for shipment. Each box weighs 2 pounds. Each widget weighs 3 pounds. Write an algebraic expression that represents the combined weights of a box and the widgets.

9. Solve. $7x - 4 = 31$

10. Simplify. $7(x - 3) - 4(x - 3)$

11. Which is a point that lies on the graph of the equation: $2x - y = 8$?
    $(3, -2), (-3, -2), (-2, 6), (-2, -6)$

12. A triangle has vertex coordinates $A(0, 0)$, $B(3, -4)$, and $C(-2, 6)$. Find the coordinates of A', B', and C' after a rotation of $180°$ about the origin.

13. Translate the triangle below 4 units to the left and 3 units up. What are the coordinates of the image of the translation?

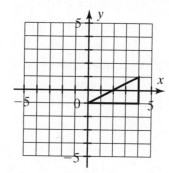

14. Determine whether $\sqrt{90}$ is rational or irrational. Explain your answer.

15. Find the missing side length of a right triangle with legs 5 and 6. Round to the nearest tenth if necessary.

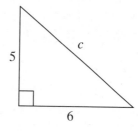

16. A bottle contained $3\frac{1}{4}$ oz of balsamic vinegar. Then $1\frac{3}{4}$ oz of the vinegar was poured into a measuring cup. How much was left in the bottle?

17. Write 0.35 as a fraction in simplest form.

18. Solve. $x - \frac{1}{2} = \frac{4}{6}$

19. What unit rate is equivalent to a rate of 165 miles in 3 hours?

20. At a fruit and vegetable stand, 5 pounds of peaches cost $7.80. How much will 3 pounds of peaches cost?

21. A maple tree casts a shadow 45 ft long. At the same time, a 40-ft-tall oak tree casts a shadow which is 60 ft long. Explain how you can use similar triangles to find the height of the tree. Then find the height of the tree.

22. Find the interest earned in a $1,200 savings account at a simple interest rate of $6\frac{1}{2}$% for 11 years.

23. 18,000 m = _?_ km

24. Solve the proportion. $\frac{14}{96} = \frac{p}{24}$

25. Write the equation you would use to solve the problem. Then solve the problem. 89 is 16% of what number? (Round to the nearest thousandth if necesssary.)

26. What is the sale price of an item having a regular price of $135 with a discount rate of 12% applied to it?

27. Estimate. 48% of 140

28. What is the final price of a $90.90 radio with a price increase of 10%?

29. Cousins Electronics buys a certain TV for $1,000 and sells it for $1,950. What is the percent of markup?

30. Find the product and write the answer in scientific notation.
$(3.2 \times 10^4) \cdot (5.6 \times 10^3)$

31. The distance from Earth to the sun is 9.6×10^7 miles. Write the number in standard form.

32. Write $\frac{-4^7}{-4^0}$ with one base and one exponent.

33. Simplify the expression $(2p^0 q^{4-5})^{3-4}$.

34. Explain why the triangles are congruent.

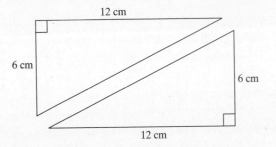

35. Find the area of the polygon.

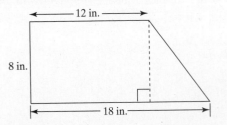

36. If $\overleftrightarrow{AB}$ and $\overleftrightarrow{CD}$ are parallel, what do you know about the measures of $\angle 1$ and $\angle 2$?

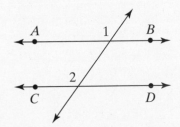

37. What is the measure of the complement of an angle with a measure of 16°?

Final Test (continued)

Chapters 1–12

38. Find the sum of the angles in this polygon.

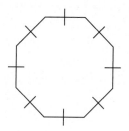

39. Find the volume of the prism.

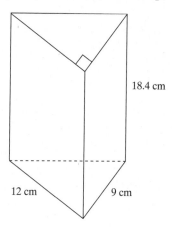

40. Find the surface area of the cylinder. Use 3.14 for π.

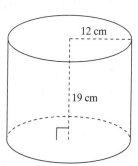

41. Calculate the volume of the pyramid.

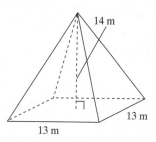

42. Identify the solid formed by the net shown.

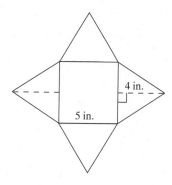

43. Find the volume of the rectangular prism after a dilation by a scale factor of 3.

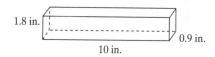

44. Name a type of data-display graph that displays data according to frequency.

45. What is the mean of the data in this stem-and-leaf diagram?

Stem	Leaf
6	0 2 4 5 6
5	2 2 3 3 4 5
4	1 2 5 8 8

Key $5|2 = 52$

46. What is the lower quartile of the data in this box-and-whisker plot?

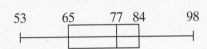

Scores on a
Social Studies Test

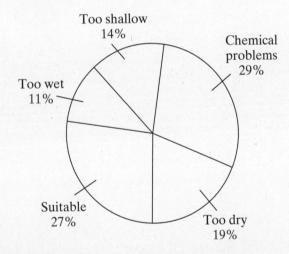

47. A scatterplot compared times for a race and time spent conditioning. What type of trend would you expect?

48. The circle graph shows data on the suitability of land for farming. What percentage of the land is too dry or too shallow?

49. A lunch menu consists of 3 different kinds of sandwiches, 3 different kinds of soup, and 5 different drinks. How many choices are there for ordering a sandwich, a bowl of soup, and a drink?

50. A committee consists of four members. If there are three men and seven women available to serve on the committee, how many different committees can be formed?

51. A silverware drawer contains 40 utensils: 15 knives, 12 spoons, and 13 forks. A utensil is chosen at random, then returned to the drawer. Another person selects a utensil at random from the drawer. Find the probability that both utensils are spoons.

52. A family is staying at a hotel with 8 floors. There are no guest rooms on the first two floors. What is the probability that the family's room is *not* on the top floor?

53. You want to conduct a survey to find out how customers feel about a bus service. How can you survey a random sample?

54. Use the function rule $f(x) = 5x - 8$ to find $f(-4)$.

55. A sequence has a common ratio of $\frac{2}{3}$ and first term of 189. Find the next three terms.

56. Add.
$$c^2 - 2c - 5$$
$$+ \quad\quad 3c + 6$$

57. Subtract.
$$(3r^3 + 6r^2 - 5r + 7)$$
$$- \ (r^3 + 6r^2 - \ r + 2)$$

58. Write the rule that relates x and y in the table.

x	1	2	3	4	5
y	6	7	8	9	10

Name _____ Class _____ Date _____

Final Test

Form D

Chapters 1–12

1. Evaluate the expression $x(4 + 5y)$ for $x = 3$ and $y = 2.4$.

2. Simplify. $\dfrac{2 + 3(8 - 2)}{(-2)(-3) - 8}$

3. What is the median of this data set?
   $16, 13, 11, 16, 10, 17, 15$

4. Order from least to greatest.
   $-19, 0, 17, 20, -21$

5. Simplify. $(-25) - (-7) - 7$

6. Solve. $z - 3 \geq 12$

7. A scoop of ice cream is $1.50. Each topping costs $.15. Write an algebraic expression representing the cost of a scoop of ice cream with x toppings.

8. Solve. $12w - 11 = 25$

9. Simplify. $9(x - 1) - 2(x - 1)$

10. Which ordered pair is a solution of the equation $5x + 3y = 13$?
    $(5, -4), (5, -3), (-3, 5), (-4, 5)$

11. A triangle has vertex coordinates $X(0, 0)$, $Y(2, 3)$, and $Z(-1, 4)$. Find the coordinates of X', Y', and Z' after a rotation of $180°$ about the origin.

12. Translate the triangle below 5 units to the left and 1 unit up. What are the coordinates of the image of the translation?

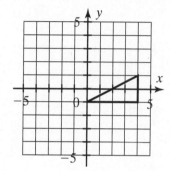

13. Identify $\sqrt{48}$ as rational or irrational. Explain your answer.

14. Find the length of the missing side of the triangle. Round to the nearest tenth if necessary.

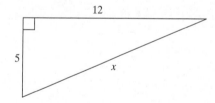

15. Brent has a board $2\frac{11}{12}$ feet long. He needs a board $3\frac{1}{6}$ feet long. How much longer does Brent's board need to be?

16. Write 0.45 as a fraction in lowest terms.

17. Solve. $N + \frac{1}{3} = \frac{4}{5}$

18. A flower shop sells 12 roses for $18.00. How much do they charge for 18 roses?

29. Explain why the triangles are congruent.

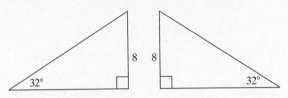

19. A tree casts a shadow of 100 feet, while a 5-foot person casts a shadow of 20 feet. How can you use similar triangles to find the height of the tree?

20. Solve the proportion. $\frac{12}{30} = \frac{18}{m}$

30. Find the area of the figure below.

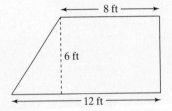

21. Write the equation you would use to solve the problem. Then solve the problem. What is 26% of 59?

22. What is the sale price of a $93 item being discounted by 30%?

31. Line *c* is parallel to line *d*. Name the interior angles below.

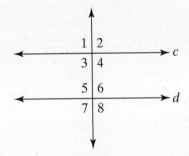

23. Estimate. 30% of 507

24. Computer Depot buys a certain computer for $2,000 and sells it for $2,750. What is the percent of increase?

25. Find the product and write the answer in scientific notation.
$(2.3 \times 10^3) \cdot (4.1 \times 10^2)$

26. The approximate diameter of a cowpox virus is written as 2.5×10^{-7} m in scientific notation. How should this number be written in standard notation?

32. What is the measure of the supplement of an angle with a measure of 41°?

33. What is the sum of the measures of all angles in a hexagon?

27. Write $\frac{(-6)^{11}}{(-6)^0}$ with one base and one exponent.

28. Simplify the expression. $(3p^0q^4)^3$

Final Test

Form D

Chapters 1–12

34. Find the surface area of the prism.

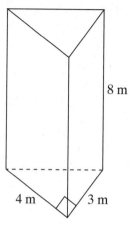

8 m

4 m   3 m

35. Find the volume of the cylindrical water bottle. Use $\pi = 3.14$.

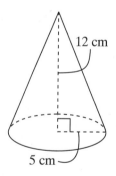

9 mm

35 mm

36. Find the volume of the cone. Use $\pi = 3.14$.

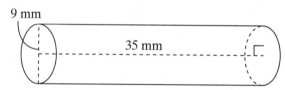

12 cm

5 cm

37. Identify the solid formed by this net.

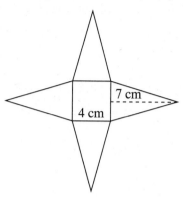

7 cm

4 cm

38. Find the volume of the rectangular prism after a dilation by a scale factor of 2.

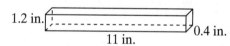

1.2 in.

11 in.

0.4 in.

39. Identify the mean in the data below.

Stem	Leaf
14	0 1 5 8
15	0 3 7
16	2 3 4 4 6 8
17	1 2 7 9

40. What is the upper quartile of the data in this box-and-whisker plot?

Scores on a
Social Studies Test

53   65   77 84   98

41. A scatterplot compared test grades and study time. What type of trend would you expect?

42. The circle graph shows data on the suitability of land for farming. What percentage of the land is too wet or too shallow?

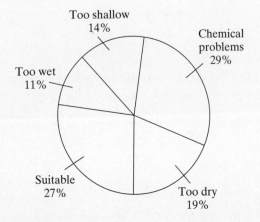

Too shallow
14%

Chemical problems
29%

Too wet
11%

Suitable
27%

Too dry
19%

43. Ms. Wong is redecorating her office. She has a choice of 3 colors of paint, 4 kinds of curtains, and 4 colors of carpet. How many different ways are there to redecorate?

44. How many ways can a president and vice-president be chosen from the 12-member math team?

45. A box contains 3 red pencils and 2 blue pencils. Two pencils are taken at random from the box in succession, without replacement. If the first pencil is red, what is the probability that the second pencil is red?

46. From a barrel of colored marbles, you randomly select 7 blue, 5 yellow, 8 red, 4 green, and 6 purple. Find the experimental probability of randomly selecting a marble that is NOT green.

47. You want to conduct a survey to find out how taxi drivers are affected by road construction. How can you survey a random sample?

48. A sequence has a common ratio of $\frac{2}{3}$ and first term of 162. Find the next three terms.

49. Add. $\quad 2q^3 - q + 3$
$$+ \qquad 7q + 9$$

50. Subtract. $\quad (3v^3 + 2v^2 - v + 1)$
$$- (2v^3 + 2v^2 - 3v - 8)$$

51. Write the rule that relates x and y in the table.

x	1	2	3	4	5
y	3	6	9	12	15

Final Test

Form E

Chapters 1–12

1. Evaluate the expression $x(22 - 5y)$ for $x = 3$ and $y = 2.2$.

2. Simplify. $72 \div 8 - 1 + 6 \cdot 2 - 20$

3. Find the median for the ages of a group of friends.
   33   34   59   49   43   29   40   59

4. Order from least to greatest.
   $-5, -101, 88, 36, -77$

5. Subtract. $200 - (-100) - 59 - (-6) - 1$

6. Solve. $p + 3 \le 24$

7. Gretchen boxes widgets for shipment. Each box weighs 2 pounds. Each widget weighs 3 pounds. Write an algebraic expression that represents the combined weights of a box and the widgets.

8. Solve. $7x - 4 = 31$

9. Simplify. $7(x - 3) - 4(x - 3)$

10. Which is a point that lies on the graph of the equation: $2x - y = 8$?
    $(3, -2), (-3, -2), (-2, 6), (-2, -6)$

11. A triangle has vertex coordinates $A(0, 0)$, $B(3, -4)$, and $C(-2, 6)$. Find the coordinates of A', B', and C' after a rotation of $180°$ about the origin.

12. Translate the triangle below 4 units to the left and 3 units up. What are the coordinates of the image of the translation?

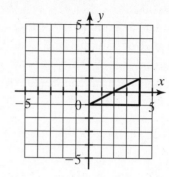

13. Determine whether $\sqrt{90}$ is rational or irrational. Explain your answer.

14. Find the missing side length of a right triangle with legs 5 and 6. Round to the nearest tenth if necessary.

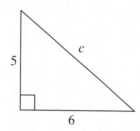

15. A bottle contained $3\frac{1}{4}$ oz of balsamic vinegar. Then $1\frac{3}{4}$ oz of the vinegar was poured into a measuring cup. How much was left in the bottle?

16. Write 0.35 as a fraction in lowest terms.

17. Solve. $x - \frac{1}{2} = \frac{4}{6}$

18. At a fruit and vegetable stand, 5 pounds of peaches cost $7.80. How much will 3 pounds of peaches cost?

19. A maple tree casts a shadow 45 ft long. At the same time, a 40-ft-tall oak tree casts a shadow which is 60 ft long. How can you use similar triangles to find the height of the tree?

20. Solve the proportion. $\frac{14}{96} = \frac{p}{24}$

21. Write the equation you would use to solve the problem. Then solve the problem. 89 is 16% of what number? (Round to the nearest thousandth if necesssary.)

22. What is the sale price of an item having a regular price of $135 with a discount rate of 12% applied to it?

23. Estimate. 48% of 140

24. Cousins Electronics buys a certain TV for $1,000 and sells it for $1,950. What is the percent increase?

25. Find the product and write the answer in scientific notation.
$(3.2 \times 10^4) \cdot (5.6 \times 10^3)$

26. The distance from Earth to the sun is 9.6×10^7 miles. Write the number in standard form.

27. Write $\frac{-4^7}{-4^0}$ with one base and one exponent.

28. Simplify the expression $(2p^0 q^{4-5})^{3-4}$.

29. Explain why the triangles are congruent.

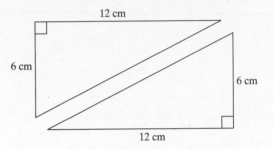

30. Find the area of the polygon.

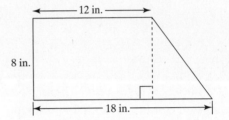

31. If $\overleftrightarrow{AB}$ and $\overleftrightarrow{CD}$ are parallel, what do you know about the measures of $\angle 1$ and $\angle 2$?

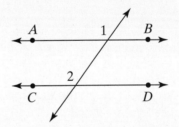

32. What is the measure of the complement of an angle with a measure of 16°?

33. Find the sum of the angles in this polygon.

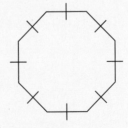

Form E

34. Find the volume of the prism.

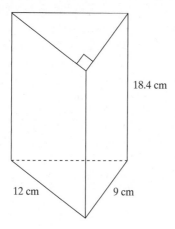

35. Find the surface area of the cylinder. Use $\pi = 3.14$.

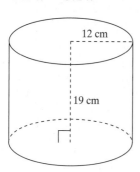

36. Calculate the volume of the pyramid.

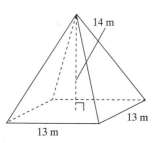

37. Identify the solid formed by the net shown.

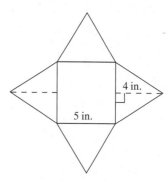

38. Find the volume of the rectangular prism after a dilation by a scale factor of 3.

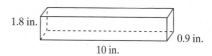

39. What is the mean of the data in this stem-and-leaf diagram?

Stem	Leaf
6	0 2 4 5 6
5	2 2 3 3 4 5
4	1 2 5 8 8

Key   5 | 2 = 52

40. What is the lower quartile of the data in this box-and-whisker plot?

Scores on a
Social Studies Test

53   65   77 84   98

41. A scatterplot compared times for a race and time spent conditioning. What type of trend would you expect?

42. The circle graph shows data on the suitability of land for farming. What percentage of the land is too dry or too shallow?

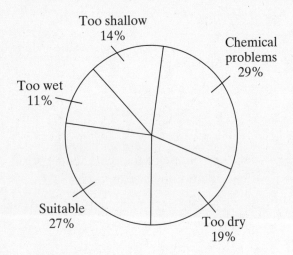

Too shallow 14%

Chemical problems 29%

Too wet 11%

Suitable 27%

Too dry 19%

43. A lunch menu consists of 3 different kinds of sandwiches, 3 different kinds of soup, and 5 different drinks. How many choices are there for ordering a sandwich, a bowl of soup, and a drink?

44. A committee consists of four members. If there are three men and seven women available to serve on the committee, how many different committees can be formed?

45. A silverware drawer contains 40 utensils: 15 knives, 12 spoons, and 13 forks. A utensil is chosen at random, then returned to the drawer. Another person selects a utensil at random from the drawer. Find the probability that both utensils are spoons.

46. A family is staying at a hotel with 8 floors. There are no guest rooms on the first two floors. What is the probability that the family's room is *not* on the top floor?

47. You want to conduct a survey to find out how customers feel about a bus service. How can you survey a random sample?

48. A sequence has a common ratio of $\frac{2}{3}$ and first term of 189. Find the next three terms.

49. Add.
$$
\begin{array}{r}
c^2 - 2c - 5 \\
+ \quad\quad 3c + 6 \\
\hline
\end{array}
$$

50. Subtract.
$$
\begin{array}{r}
(3r^3 + 6r^2 - 5r + 7) \\
- \quad (r^3 + 6r^2 - \ \ r + 2) \\
\hline
\end{array}
$$

51. Write the rule that relates x and y in the table.

x	1	2	3	4	5
y	6	7	8	9	10

Writing Gridded Responses

Exercises

Mark your answers on the grid for each exercise.

1. Amanda is 14 cm taller than her sister, Rachel. The sum of their heights is 96 cm. How many centimeters tall is Amanda?

2. The record high temperature for January in Cleveland, OH was 73°F in 1950. The record low temperature for January, −20°F, occurred in 1994. What is the difference (in degrees) between these temperatures?

3. Evaluate $|7 - 5h|$ for $h = 9$.

4. Peaches were on sale for $1.49 per pound. Zoe bought three pounds and gave the cashier a $10 bill. How much change, in dollars, does Zoe receive?

5. Simplify. $\dfrac{-128}{-4}$

6. The area of a rectangle is 72 cm². The length is 6 cm greater than the width. How many centimeters long is the rectangle?

Writing Short Responses

Exercises

Use the scoring rubric shown to answer each question.

> **Scoring Rubric**
>
> **2** The equation and solution are correct.
>
> **1** There is no equation, but there is a method to show the correct solution.
>
> **1** There is an equation and a solution but they contain minor errors.
>
> **0** There is no response, or the solution is completely incorrect.

A carpet cleaning service charges a flat fee of $50 plus $15 per room to clean the carpet in a home. A family paid $185 to have their carpet cleaned. Write and solve an equation to find out how many rooms they have.

2 points	1 point	0 points
Let x = the number of rooms. $$50 + 15x = 185$$ $$15x = 135$$ $$\frac{15x}{15} = \frac{135}{15}$$ $$x = 9$$ The family has 9 rooms.	$185 - 50 = 135$ $\frac{135}{15} = 9$ 9	$50x + 15 = 185$ $65x = 185$ $x = 2.85$ 3 rooms

1. Explain why each response above received the indicated points.

_____

_____

_____

_____

_____

_____

2. Write a two-point response for the following problem: Doreen bought three identical ceramic figurines and paid a flat fee of $12.50 to have them glazed. If her bill (before taxes) came to $39.47, how much was each figurine?

_____

_____

Writing Extended Responses
Exercises

Use the scoring rubric shown to solve the problem.

To receive full credit, you must: (1) define variables and write two correct linear equations, (2) graph each equation with the correct slope and *y*-intercept, and (3) find the break-even point. The number of points for different types of answers is as follows.

Scoring Rubric

4 The equations, the graphs, and the solution are correct.

3 The equations and the graphs are correct, but the solution is incorrect.

2 There are equations, graphs, and a solution, some of which have minor errors in them.

1 The variables are chosen and defined. The equations, the graphs, and the solution have many flaws in them.

0 There is no response, the answer is completely incorrect, or it is a correct response but no procedure is shown.

The Student Council at North High School is selling picture frames for Spirit Day. The frames cost $1.50 each and a flat fee of $10.50 for shipping. The Student Council plans to sell the frames for $2.25 each. Write the equations for expenses and income. Solve the system by graphing to find how many picture frames they must sell to break even.

1. Write a 4-point solution to this problem.

_____

_____

_____

2. How many points should a student receive for the solution shown at the right? Explain.

$$10.50 \div 0.75 = 14$$
The answer is 14.

_____

_____

Using a Variable
Exercises

Define a variable. Then, write and solve an equation for each problem.

1. In a bag, the ratio of red marbles to blue marbles is 9 to 21.
   The bag contains 30 red marbles. How many blue marbles
   are in the bag?

   _____

2. The Sampson family is building a playhouse. The scale of their
   blueprint is 2.5 cm : 12 ft. The playhouse will be 24 ft wide and 30
   ft long. Find the dimensions on the blueprint.

   _____

   _____

3. A 3 ft high fire hydrant casts a 5 ft long shadow. Gena is standing
   nearby and casts an 8.5 ft long shadow. How tall is Gena?

   _____

4. A family is on a 520-mi road trip. They have driven 195 mi in
   3 hours. If they continue driving at this rate, how long will it take
   them to drive the entire 520 mi?

   _____

5. An architect's drawing of a museum is 18 cm wide by 28 cm long.
   The actual building is going to be 45 m wide. How long will the
   building be?

   _____

6. A painter is mixing paint. The directions say to mix red, blue, and
   yellow paint in a ratio of 3 : 7 : 6. He needs a gallon of paint. How
   many ounces of each color does the painter need?

   _____

   _____

   _____

7. A seamstress can make two dresses in nine hours.

   a. At this rate, how long will it take her to make seven dresses?

   _____

   b. How many dresses can she make in 15 hours?

   _____

Estimating the Answer

Exercises

Estimate each answer.

1. Ted collects rare gold coins. He bought one coin in his collection for $32.85. Five years later, the coin was worth $54.79. Use estimating to find the percent of increase in the value of the coin.

   A. 21.94%   **B.** 40%   **C.** 50%   **D.** $66\frac{2}{3}$ %

2. Georgianne wants to leave a 20% tip for her $45 haircut. Estimate how much she should tip her hairdresser.

   F. $54   **G.** $9   **H.** $7   **J.** $5

3. In a recent school election, 76% of the students voted for the winning candidate for student council treasurer. If 392 students voted, how many voted for the winning candidate?

   A. 325   **B.** 300   **C.** 275   **D.** 250

4. Estimate 28% of 621.

   F. 280   **G.** 200   **H.** 195   **J.** 180

5. A basketball player made 88% of 48 free-throw attempts in one season. About how many free-throws did the player successfully make during the season?

   A. 45   **B.** 35   **C.** 32   **D.** 9

6. Estimate the selling price of a video game if the percent of markup is 24% and the store's cost is $38.99.

   F. $40   **G.** $50   **H.** $60   **J.** $40

7. Which percent is closest to $\frac{78}{321}$?

   A. 78%   **B.** 40%   **C.** 25%   **D.** $33\frac{1}{3}$ %

8. Jiroko deposits $3,046 into a savings account that earns 6.85% simple interest. Approximately how much money will be in the account at the end of 3 years?

   F. $6,320   **G.** $3,640   **H.** $3,230   **J.** $3,000

9. On the first day of a new release, a video store rented out 72% of its 89 copies of the movie. Approximately how many copies did the video store rent?

   A. 45   **B.** 57   **C.** 63   **D.** 72

10. Estimate the final cost of a CD that costs $12.99 if the tax rate is 5.25%

    F. $13.65   **G.** $14.00   **H.** $15.00   **I.** $15.45

Reading for Understanding

Exercises

Use the passage for the following exercises.

> Since the earliest centuries, artists, musicians, architects, and mathematicians have been intrigued by a figure known as "The Golden Rectangle." The rectangle's pleasant shape has made it popular. A rectangle is a Golden Rectangle if the ratio of its larger side to its smaller side is 1.618 to 1.
>
> Famous artists, including Piet Mondrian, Seurat, and Leonardo Da Vinci, used the Golden Rectangle in their paintings. In music, the Mozart sonatas and Beethoven's Fifth Symphony have been linked to the Golden Rectangle. On the famed Stradivarius violins, placement of the sound holes is also related to the Golden Rectangle.
>
> Most experts agree that the ancient Greek civilization used the Golden Rectangle when building the Parthenon, among other buildings. Finally, the ratio of the base and the height of the ancient Egyptian pyramids is also close to the ratio of the Golden Rectangle.

1. The shorter side of a window is 36 in. The window is shaped like a Golden Rectangle. Find the length of the longer side of the window. Round your answer to the nearest hundredth.

   _____

2. The longer edge of a picture frame is 18 in. The picture frame is shaped like a Golden Rectangle. What is the length of the shorter edge of the picture frame? Round your answer to the nearest hundredth.

   _____

3. The dimensions of a computer screen are 28 cm by 21 cm. Is the shape of the computer screen a Golden Rectangle? Explain.

   _____

   _____

   _____

   _____

Drawing a Picture
Exercises

Draw a picture to help you solve each problem.

1. In Nathan's neighborhood, the library (L), the school (S), and the grocery store (G) lie on a straight road in that order. The distance from S to G is 5 times the distance from L to S. The distance from L to G is 28 more than 4 times the distance from L to S. What is the distance between the library and the school?

   _____

2. $R(3, 4)$, $S(8, 4)$, and $T(1, 1)$ are three vertices of two parallelograms, in no particular order. Find the coordinates of U, the fourth vertex in each parallelogram.

   _____

   _____

3. Quadrilateral $JKLM$ has vertices $J(1, 7)$, $K(6, 0)$, $L(1, -7)$ and $M(-4, 0)$. What is the best name for the quadrilateral?

   _____

4. The sides of a parallelogram and one of its diagonals form two isosceles triangles. Must the parallelogram be a rhombus?

   _____

5. Maple Street is parallel to Elm Street. Oak Street is perpendicular to Maple Street. Chestnut Street is perpendicular to Elm Street. Are Chestnut Street and Oak Street parallel?

   _____

6. The light from a night watchman's tower extends 440 yd in all directions. What is the area covered by the night watchman's light? Use 3.14 for π and round to the nearest square yard.

   _____

7. Natalie rides her bike from her house to her friend Jon's house. She rides 5 blocks north, 2 blocks east, 3 blocks north, then 4 blocks east. A path goes straight from her house to Jon's house. How many blocks would she have walked if she had taken the path?

   _____

8. The length of a rectangle is 9 more than 4 times the width. The perimeter of the rectangle is 128 cm. Find the length and width.

   _____

Eliminating Answers

Exercises

Use the following multiple choice question to answer exercises 1–2.

What is the volume of a square pyramid with a base edge length of 9 ft and a height of 17 ft?

   A. 1,377 ft   **B.** 459 ft^2 **C.** 306 ft^3 **D.** 459 ft^3

1. Which answer choices can be eliminated? Why?

       _____

       _____

       _____

2. Find the correct answer choice. _____

Solve each multiple choice question by eliminating answers.

3. The volume of a cube is 24 m^3. The lengths of the sides are increased by a scale factor of $\frac{6}{5}$. What is the volume of the new cube?

   F. 41.472 m^3 **G.** 192 m^3 **H.** 28.8 m^3 **J.** 34.56 m^3

4. What is the surface area of a cylinder with a radius of 5 cm and a height of 14 m?

   A. 710π m^3 **B.** 190π m^3 **C.** 190π m^2 **D.** 190 m^2

5. A box measuring 5-in.-by-2-in.-by-7 in. is packed inside a gift box that is an 8-in. cube. How much space is left inside for packing materials?

   F. 512 in.^{3} **G.** 442 in.^{3} **H.** 118 in.^{3} **J.** 70 in.^{3}

6. A round table has a diameter of 3 ft. What size tablecloth is needed to have one foot of overhang all around the table?

   A. 19.625 ft^2 **B.** 7.065 ft^2 **C.** 15.7 ft^2 **D.** 12.56 ft^2

7. The surface area of a rectangular prism is 126 in.^{2} The surface area of a similar rectangular prism is 224 in.^{2} What is the ratio of corresponding dimensions of the small prism to the large prism?

   F. $\frac{16}{9}$ **G.** $\frac{4}{3}$ **H.** $\frac{9}{16}$ **J.** $\frac{3}{4}$

Measuring to Solve
Exercises

Use a ruler to answer each question. Round to the nearest tenth, if necessary.

1. The net at the right forms a square prism. Measure its dimensions in centimeters.

   Find the surface area of the prism.

   _____

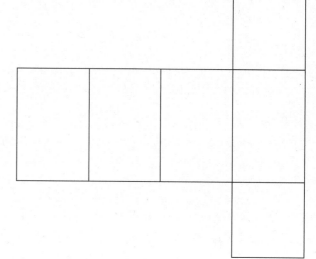

2. The net at the right forms a triangular pyramid. Measure its dimensions in centimeters.

   Find the surface area of the triangular pyramid.

   _____

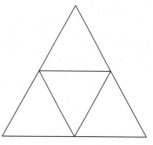

3. The net at the right forms a cylinder. Measure its dimensions in centimeters. Use 3.14 for π. Find the surface area of the cylinder.

   _____

Answering the Question Asked

Exercises

Read each question carefully. Then solve.

1. James is choosing 4 books from his shelf to take on vacation. His shelf contains 9 books. How many different ways can James choose the books?

   A. 3,024   **B.** 126   **C.** 120   **D.** 36

2. A spinner numbered from one to eight is divided into eight equal sections. What is the probability of spinning a one or an eight?

   F. $\frac{1}{16}$ **G.** $\frac{1}{64}$ **H.** 12.5%   **J.** 25%

3. A bag contains 7 green marbles, 11 red marbles, and 2 blue marbles. What is the probability of *not* drawing a red marble?

   A. 45%   **B.** 40%   **C.** 35%   **D.** 10%

4. A basket of fruit contains 4 apples, 6 oranges, and 5 plums. Deanna chooses 2 pieces of fruit without replacing her first choice. What is the probability she will first choose an orange, then a plum?

   F. $\frac{2}{5}$ **G.** $\frac{1}{3}$ **H.** $\frac{1}{7}$ **J.** $\frac{2}{15}$

5. You deposit $1,500 into an account that pays 4.5% interest compounded annually. How much is in the account at the end of 4 years?

   A. $1,788.78   **B.** $1,770.00   **C.** $1,567.50   **D.** $270.00

6. A jewelry store sells watches, rings, and necklaces. Over time, the jeweler has found that 40% of her customers buy watches and 25% buy necklaces. What is the probability that a person will buy either a watch or a necklace?

   F. 0.65   **G.** 0.40   **H.** 0.35   **J.** 0.25

7. Each letter in the word GEOMETRY appears on a card. You choose a card at random and then replace it. Then you choose a second card. What is the probability that you will draw 2 E's?

   A. $\frac{1}{16}$ **B.** $\frac{2}{15}$ **C.** $\frac{1}{8}$ **D.** $\frac{1}{4}$

8. Fourteen schools compete in a band competition. Gold, silver, and bronze medals are awarded for first, second, and third place. How many different arrangements of winners can there be?

   F. 2,744   **H.** 2,184   **G.** 364   **J.** 39

Interpreting Data

Exercises

Use the graphs at the right to answer each question.

1. The graph shows the percent of time Colin spends practicing each sport. If he has 2 hours to spend practicing, how many minutes will he spend practicing soccer?

   A. 18   **B.** 24
   C. 40   **D.** 48

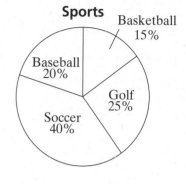

Sports

Basketball 15%
Baseball 20%
Golf 25%
Soccer 40%

2. If Colin has 3.5 hours to spend practicing, how many minutes will he spend practicing baseball?

   F. 42   **G.** 84
   H. 40   **J.** 20

3. Predict the weight for a person who is 55 inches tall.

   A. 45 pounds

   B. 55 pounds

   C. 90 pounds

   D. 120 pounds

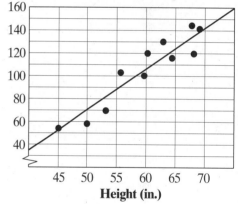

Height and Weight

Height (in.)

4. Which statement is NOT supported by the information in the line graph at the right?

   F. As height increases, so does weight.

   G. This graph has a positive trend.

   H. People lose weight as they grow taller.

   J. As a person grows taller, they weigh more.

5. What is the mode of the scores shown in the stem-and-leaf plot at the right?

   A. 4   **B.** 77
   C. 84   **D.** 102

6. What is the range of the scores shown in the stem-and-leaf plot at the right?

   F. 1   **G.** 23
   H. 31   **J.** 84

Golf Scores

7	1 1 2 3 5 7 7 8
8	2 2 3 4 4 4 5 6 8 8 9
9	1 3 4 5 5
10	1 1 2

Key: 7 | 1 means 71

Working Backward

Exercises

Solve each of the following by working backward.

1. Solve for x. $5x + 4 = 29$

   A. $x = 2$ **B.** $x = 5$ **C.** $x = 7$ **D.** $x = 12$

2. Consider the function $f(x) = 3x - 7$. What value of x will make $f(x) = 20$?

   F. 53   **G.** 9   **H.** -36 **J.** -80

3. The area of a circle is 15.9 mm². What is the diameter of the circle?

   A. 4.5 mm   **B.** 3.14 mm   **C.** 2.25 mm   **D.** 1.05 mm

4. The base of a rectangular prism has a length of 9 in. and a width of 7 in. The volume of the prism is 787.5 in.³. What is the height of the prism?

   F. 87.5 in.   **G.** 63 in.   **H.** 12.5 in.   **J.** 7.875 in.

5. If $x^3 = 64$, find the value of $\frac{x^5}{x^3}$.

   A. 1,024   **B.** 16   **C.** 8   **D.** 4

6. Which number could *not* be a value of y if $y = 5x^2 - 9$?

   F. 11   **G.** -4 **H.** -9 **J.** -10

7. The side lengths of which of the following triangles do *not* form a right triangle?

   A. 12 cm, 16 cm, 20 cm   **B.** 10 cm, 24 cm, 26 cm

   C. 8 cm, 10 cm, 12 cm   **D.** 15 cm, 20 cm, 25 cm

8. Jennie's average after four math tests is an 85. What must Jennie score on the fifth test to raise her grade to an 87?

   F. 100   **G.** 95   **H.** 91   **J.** 87

9. Which ordered pair lies on the line $y = 11x - 13$?

   A. $(2, 9)$ **B.** $(-13, 0)$ **C.** $(0, 11)$ **D.** $(1, 2)$

10. You start an exercise program. You begin by walking 1.5 mi the first day and increase your distance by 0.25 mi per day. How many miles do you walk on the 7th day?

    F. 1.75 mi   **G.** 3 mi   **H.** 3.25 mi   **J.** 3.5 mi

NAEP Practice Test

1. Kelly is buying snacks for the school dance. She needs 15 bags of chips and 11 bags of pretzels. Each bag of chips costs $4.39 and each bag of pretzels costs $3.89. Which expression gives Kelly the most accurate estimation of the total cost of snacks for the dance?

   A $(4 + 4) \cdot (11 + 15)$

   B $(3 \times 11) + (4 \times 15)$

   C $(4 \times 11) + (4 \times 15)$

   D $(3 + 4) \cdot (10 + 15)$

   E $(3 \times 11) + (3 \times 15)$

2. Between which two consecutive whole numbers does the $\sqrt{209}$ lie?

   A 11 and 12

   B 12 and 13

   C 13 and 14

   D 14 and 15

   E 15 and 16

3. The distance from Baltimore, MD, to Washington, D. C., is approximately 36 miles. If 1 kilometer is approximately 0.621 miles, about how many kilometers is it from Baltimore to Washington D. C.?

   A 20 kilometers

   B 22 kilometers

   C 48 kilometers

   D 55 kilometers

   E 58 kilometers

4. At the 8th grade graduation party there were five rectangular carrot cakes, one for each middle school team. The cakes were cut into equal pieces in different ways as shown. The shaded parts of each cake were left over. Which cake had the greatest fraction of the original cake left over?

A
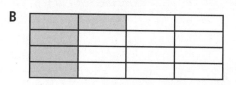

B
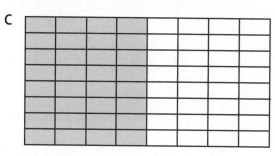

C

D
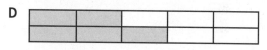

E
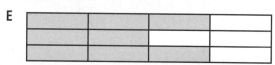

5. Which data set has a mean equal to its median?

   A 1, 8, 7, 6, 4, 3, 5, 2

   B 10, 3, 8, 5, 7, 7, 10, 4

   C 1, 12, 3, 3, 3, 10, 9, 11

   D 7, 7, 9, 4, 3, 6, 1, 1

   E 27, 19, 31, –5, 3, 3, 17, 7

6. Chelsea's last seven test scores are 89, 95, 80, 93, 89, 86, and 92. She has one more test before the end of the grading period. In order to have an average of at least 90 for the grading period, what is the lowest score Chelsea can get on the final test?

A 95

B 96

C 97

D 98

E 99

7. Keesha has half as many quarters as dimes and twice as many quarters as nickels. What expression represents the number of coins Keesha has?

A $d + \frac{d}{2} + \frac{2d}{4}$

B $12d + 6n + 3q$

C $d + \frac{q}{2} + 2n$

D $d + \frac{d}{2} + \frac{(d/2)}{2}$

E $8 + 4 + 2$

8. What is the value of the expression $5x^2 - 7(x + y) - y$ if $x = -4$ and $y = 6$?

A -4

B 4

C 24

D 60

E 170

9. If $2(x + 4) = 86$, then $x =$

A -90

B 21

C 39

D 43

E 176

10. Ms. Dempsy's social studies classes are collecting canned goods for the local emergency food shelter. Their goal is to collect 2,000 cans of food. During the first week, Ms. Dempsy's 112 students collected an average of 8 cans each. Which equation shows the average number of cans, c, that each student must still collect?

A $c = 2,000 - (8 \times 112)$

B $c = \frac{2,000}{(112 - 8)}$

C $2,000 = 112(c + 8)$

D $2,000 = 8(112 + c)$

E $112c = \frac{2,000}{8}$

11. Arwin and John are trying to solve the equation $2x + 5 - x = 7 + x$. Arwin says they first need to subtract x from the right-hand side of the equation and add x to the left-hand side. What should John say to Arwin to show her that she's wrong?

A No, you should add x to both sides of the equation.

B No, you shouldn't subtract x from either side of the equation.

C No, you should add x to the right side of the equation.

D No, you should subtract x from both sides of the equation.

E No, you should add 5 to both sides of the equation.

GO ON

12. If $-8 + 9x = 2 + 14x$, then $x =$

  A -3 **B** -2

  C 2 **D** 3

  E 6

13. Which equation represents the model?

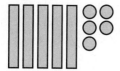

  A $5x = 19$

  B $5x + 2 = 2x + 19$

  C $5x - 2 = 2x - 19$

  D $5x - 5 = 2x - 19$

  E $5x + 5 = 2x + 19$

14. Which inequality represents the graph?

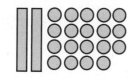

  A $x > 2$ **B** $x < 2$

  C $x \le 2$ **D** $x \ge 2$

  E $x \ne 2$

15. If $2x - 6 < 14$, which number is **not** a solution?

  A 4

  B 7

  C 8

  D 9

  E 11

16. If $6x + 11 \le 47$, then

  A $x \le 7\frac{5}{6}$

  B $x \le 6$

  C $x \ge 6$

  D $x > 36$

  E $x > 58$

17. A light-year is the distance that light travels in one year, which is approximately 5,880,000,000,000 miles. The closest star to Earth, Alpha Centauri, is 4 light-years away. How would that distance, in miles, be expressed in scientific notation?

  A 5.88×10^4

  B 5.88×4^{10}

  C 2.35×10^{13}

  D 2.35×10^{115}

  E $1.00 \times 10^{2.35}$

18. Ellie is sorting donations of greeting cards into stacks. She has 646 cards. What is the greatest number of stacks she can make if each stack has the same number of cards?

A 6
B 7
C 11
D 17
E 19

19. What is the largest prime factor of 1,496?

A 11
B 17
C 19
D 23
E 31

20. Which fraction, when simplified, does **not** equal $\frac{5}{6}$?

A $\frac{9}{12}$
B $\frac{15}{18}$
C $\frac{25}{30}$
D $\frac{30}{36}$
E $\frac{40}{48}$

21. Eric started an exercise program. He power walked $1\frac{1}{3}$ miles the first day, $2\frac{5}{8}$ miles the second day, and $3\frac{1}{6}$ miles the third day. What was Eric's total distance for the three days?

A $5\frac{5}{12}$ miles
B $5\frac{27}{24}$ miles
C $6\frac{15}{24}$ miles
D $7\frac{1}{8}$ miles
E $7\frac{25}{24}$ miles

22. A garden measures $5\frac{1}{4}$ feet by $9\frac{1}{6}$ feet. A brick border runs around the entire garden. The brick border is $\frac{7}{8}$ foot wide. What are the dimensions of the garden including the brick border?

A $6\frac{1}{8}$ feet by $10\frac{1}{24}$ feet

B $6\frac{1}{8}$ feet by $10\frac{11}{12}$ feet

C 7 feet by $10\frac{11}{12}$ feet

D 14 feet by $21\frac{5}{6}$ feet

E 7 feet by $10\frac{5}{6}$ feet

23. $2\frac{5}{8} \cdot \left(-1\frac{3}{4}\right) =$

A $-4\frac{19}{32}$
B $-4\frac{3}{8}$
C $4\frac{3}{8}$
D $4\frac{19}{32}$
E $2\frac{7}{16}$

24. $7\frac{1}{2} \div 6\frac{2}{3} =$

A $\frac{1}{8}$
B $1\frac{1}{8}$
C $13\frac{5}{6}$
D $42\frac{1}{3}$
E 50

GO ON

25. Rhonda is measuring the distance between her house and her new school. Which unit of measurement should she use?

A centimeters   **B** meters

C kilometers   **D** feet

E inches

26. Which figure has the greatest ratio of *shaded* area to *not-shaded* area?

A
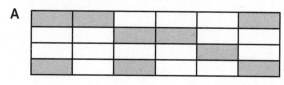

B
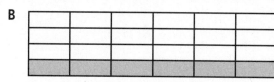

C
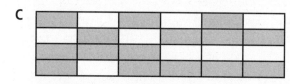

D
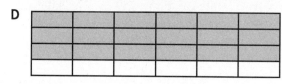

E
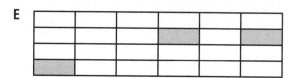

27. Cesar takes care of people's pets. He makes $3.75 for taking care of a cat, $6.25 for walking a dog, $2.35 for feeding fish, and $15.45 for taking care of a pet overnight. If Cesar does each of these jobs twice, how much does he earn?

A $24.05   **B** $25.45

C $27.80   **D** $48.10

E $55.60

28. An airplane can fly 1,372 miles in 4 hours. At the same rate, how many miles can the plane fly in 7 hours?

A 784 miles   **B** 1,715 miles

C 2,058 miles   **D** 2,401 miles

E 2,744 miles

29. If you cross multiply to solve the proportion $\frac{x}{8} = \frac{5}{23}$, which response could you use to solve the proportion?

A $23 = 5x$ **B** $23x = \frac{5}{8}$

C $(5)(23) = 8x$ **D** $(5)(8) = 23x$

E $230 = 5x$

30. If $\frac{8}{15} = \frac{32}{x}$, then $x =$

A 4   **B** $17\frac{5}{12}$

C 60   **D** 80

E 120

> GO ON

31. The top of the basketball backboard is 12 feet high, and the shadow from the pole, hoop, and backboard is 18 feet long. At the same time of day, the shadow of a telephone pole near the backboard is 45 feet long. How tall is the telephone pole?

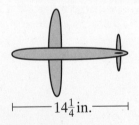

A 24 ft

B 30 ft

C 36 ft

D 48 ft

E 72 ft

32. The model airplane shown below has a scale of $\frac{3}{4}$ inch = 2 feet. What is the length of the actual plane?

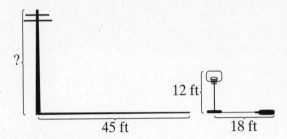

├─── $14\frac{1}{4}$ in. ───┤

A 19 feet

B $23\frac{3}{4}$ feet

C $28\frac{1}{2}$ feet

D 32 feet

E 38 feet

33. Charlie's family is building a deck on the back of their house. The plans are drawn to a scale of $\frac{1}{4}$ inch = 1 foot. What is the area of the actual deck?

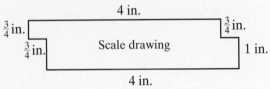

A 52 ft^2

B 104 ft^2

C 112 ft^2

D 144 ft^2

E 256 ft^2

34. There was a sidewalk sale at Mega Mall. Everything was marked down by 30%. Rodrick bought 3 pairs of jeans originally priced at $29.95 each, a shirt originally priced at $18.50, and a pair of sandals originally priced at $32.29. The sales tax in Rodrick's state is 7.25%. How much was Rodrick's total?

A $94.25

B $100.85

C $105.59

D $140.64

E $162.58

>GO ON>

Name_____ Class_____ Date_____

35. Daryl earned 426 points out of 500 points in his English class. Which percent approximately represents Daryl's points?

   A 43%   **B** 79%

   C 84%   **D** 85%

   E 117%

36. Park View Middle School has 786 students. Of the 786 students, 32% walk to school, 17% ride their bikes to school, and 8% are driven to school. The rest of the students ride the bus. Which number best approximates the number of students who ride the bus?

   A 134   **B** 197

   C 252   **D** 338

   E 448

37. Music Square buys guitars for $230 and then marks the price up 150%. The store buys guitar cases for $35 and then marks the price up by 230%. What does Music Square charge for a guitar and a case?

   A $265.00   **B** $345.00

   C $425.50   **D** $575.00

   E $690.50

38. In which figure is the measure of $\angle ABC$ equal to 152°?

A
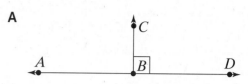

B
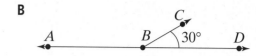

C
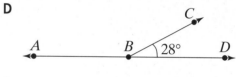

D
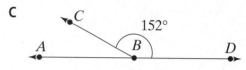

E
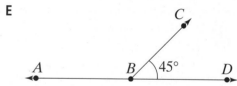

39. What kind of triangle is shown?

   A acute triangle

   B equilateral triangle

   C acute isosceles triangle

   D scalene triangle

   E right isosceles triangle

40. What is the measure of ∠R?

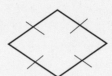

A 8°

B 10°

C 12°

D 20°

E 40°

41. What is the name of the figure shown?

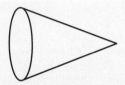

A pyramid

B cone

C cylinder

D round prism

E sphere

42. Which polygon is a rhombus?

A

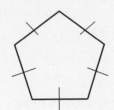

B

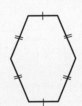

C

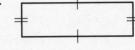

D

E

43. This figure can be made up of which combination of other figures?

A 3 triangles

B 1 triangle and 1 square

C 1 square and 2 triangles

D 1 parallelogram, 1 triangle, and 1 square

E none of the above

GO ON

NAEP Practice Test

44. What is the value of *x*?

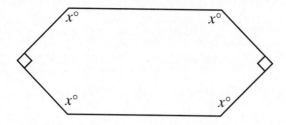

    A 45°

    B 90°

    C 106°

    D 132°

    E 135°

45. Triangles *ABC* and *RPQ* are similar. What is the length of *QR*?

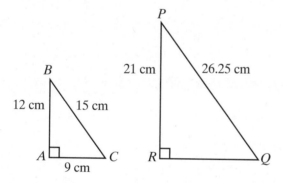

    A 3 cm

    B 4 cm

    C 15 cm

    D 15.75 cm

    E 17.5 cm

46. A circle has a circumference of 50.24 meters. What is the circle's radius? Use 3.14 for π.

    A 3.14 meters

    B 4 meters

    C 8 meters

    D 12 meters

    E 16 meters

47. A teen magazine did a survey and asked 1,200 students to choose their favorite after-school activity. Students had four choices: surfing the Internet, hanging out with friends, going to a movie, or doing homework. How many students chose going to a movie?

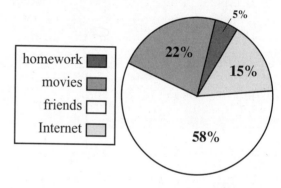

    A 60

    B 180

    C 264

    D 696

    E 960

GO ON

48. What is the area of the trapezoid?

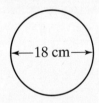

24 in.

8 in.

12 in.

A 120 square inches

B 144 square inches

C 120 square inches

D 46 square inches

E 118 square inches

49. Brody and Phillip are constructing a giant isosceles triangle out of cardboard. The base of the triangle is 7 feet and the height is 16 feet. They have 58 square feet of cardboard. How much cardboard will be left over when they are done?

A 1.75 square feet

B 2 square feet

C 8 square feet

D They don't have enough cardboard.

E none of the above

50. Volunteers are putting a new fence around the vegetable garden for the food co-op. Fencing comes in 8-foot sections and costs $20 a section. How much will it cost to fence the garden?

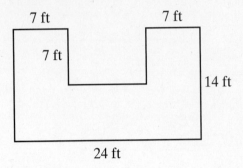

7 ft   7 ft

7 ft   14 ft

24 ft

A $160

B $190

C $240

D $280

E $340

51. What is the circumference of the circle? Use 3.14 for π.

18 cm

A 28.26 cm

B 56.52 cm

C 254.34 cm

D 254.34 cm

E 1,017.36 cm

GO ON

52. The rectangle is divided by two diagonals. Approximately how long is each diagonal?

18 m

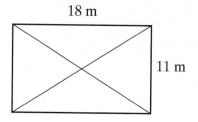

11 m

A 18.4 m   **B** 20 m

C 21.1 m   **D** 36.8 m

E 42.2 m

53. There are approximately 7.48 gallons in a cubic foot. How many gallons will this cylindrical tank hold?

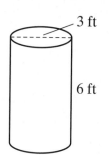

3 ft

6 ft

A 42.4 gallons   **B** 44.9 gallons

C 89.8 gallons   **D** 211.2 gallons

E 317.1 gallons

54. If the pattern continues, what will be the next number after 45?
10, 20, 15, 30, 25, 50, 45. . .

A 60   **B** 70

C 90   **D** 95

E 100

55. Which rule describes the sequence listed below for $n = 1, 2, 3, \ldots$?
$3, 5, 7, 9, 11, 13, 15, \ldots$.

A $n + \frac{n}{2}$ **B** $2n + 1$

C $n + 7$ **D** $3n \div 5$

E n^{2-n}

56. Which function represents the graph?

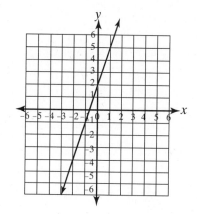

A $y = \frac{x}{3}$ **B** $y = 3x^2$

C $y = 3 + x$ **D** $y = -3x$

E $y = 3x + 2$

57. Which of the following ordered pairs is NOT a solution to $y = 2x - 3$?

A $(1, -3)$ **B** $(2, 1)$

C $(3, 3)$ **D** $(5, 7)$

E $(14, 25)$

GO ON

58. Which rule is shown by the table below?

x	y
−4	−3
−2	−1.5
0	0
2	1.5
4	3
6	4.5

A $y = 3x - 4$ **B** $y = \frac{3}{4}x$

C $y = \frac{4}{3x}$ **D** $y = 3x + 4$

E $y = \frac{x}{3} - 4$

59. Which is a graph of a linear function?

A

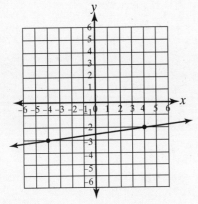

B

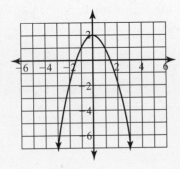

C

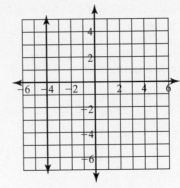

D

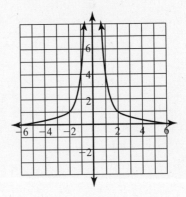

E

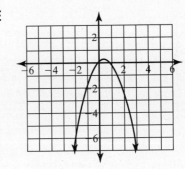

60. What type of trend would you expect to see in a scatter plot comparing the size of a tree's trunk to the tree's age?

A positive **B** negative

C opposite **D** none

E inverse

 GO ON

61. The marketing manager of an electronics store is trying to do a survey of its customers' buying habits. Which method will give her a random sample?

A Survey all the people who come to the store the first hour that it is open in the morning.

B Survey every other woman who comes into the store after 6:00 P.M.

C Survey every tenth customer for a week.

D Survey every tenth family of four that comes into the store.

E Survey every customer who comes into the store on Saturday morning.

62. Four green marbles and six blue marbles are placed in a bag. A volunteer randomly chooses one marble, keeps it, and then chooses a second marble. What is $P(\text{green and green})$?

A $\frac{5}{10}$ **B** $\frac{6}{10}$

C $\frac{1}{10}$ **D** $\frac{3}{9}$

E $\frac{2}{15}$

63. Jenna and Lara are using a spinner with four same-size sections: red, blue, yellow, and purple. The table shows the outcomes of their spins. Which statement reflects the relationship between the experimental and theoretical probability for "yellow?"

Red	𝈫𝈫 IIII
Blue	𝈫𝈫𝈫 III
Yellow	𝈫 III
Purple	𝈫𝈫𝈫𝈫

A The theoretical and experimental probabilities are the same.

B The theoretical probability is greater than the experimental probability.

C The experimental probability is greater than the theoretical probability.

D The experimental probability is always greater than the theoretical probability.

E The spinner results are always the same.

Short Constructed Response

64. Explain how you could find the 10th term of the following sequence: 3, 4, 6, 9, 13, 18 . . . .

65. Reilly wanted to get into shape so she decided to do interval training. She varied her activity. She spent 15 minutes power walking for a mile, 20 minutes jogging 2 miles, 10 minutes walking a $\frac{1}{2}$ mile, and 15 minutes walking slowly for a $\frac{1}{2}$ mile. Create a graph that shows how Reilly's rate changed throughout her workout. Explain your graph.

GO ON

66. Megan is standing 12 feet away from a basketball hoop, which is 10 feet in the air. How far is it from Megan's feet to the hoop? Round your answer to the nearest tenth.

67. You want to enclose an off-leash area for dogs with segments of a fence that are all the same length. The off-leash area is shown below.

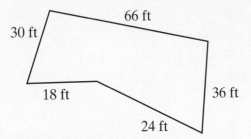

66 ft

30 ft

18 ft

36 ft

24 ft

What is the greatest length that a segment of fence can be so that the segments will fill each side without gaps? If you use segments of greatest lengths, how many segments are needed to enclose the entire off-leash area for dogs?

68. The 8th grade class had 3 days to vote on their new school colors. The graph below shows how many students chose each of the colors.

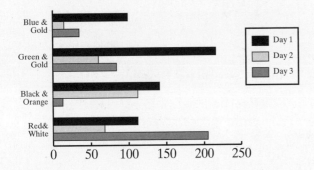

According to the graph, what colors should be chosen as the class colors? Explain.

69. Erika knows that $x < y$ and that $x^2 < y^2$. Erika claims that this means $x < 0$ and $y < 0$. Is she correct? Why or why not?

70. Faith drives 30 miles due north and 40 miles due west to travel to her friend's house. Her car gets 18 miles per gallon, and she paid $1.45 per gallon of gasoline. If she had taken a different route, she would have traveled 21 miles more. How much money did Faith save by taking the shorter route? Explain.

STOP

SAT 10 Practice Test

PS *Mathematics: Problem Solving*

Read each question. Then mark your answer on the answer sheet.

1. **Which of the following is NOT a true statement?**

   A $-12 > -15$

   B $4 > -1$

   C $-8 < -9$

   D $0 > -10$

2. **Which is listed in order from least to greatest?**

   F $\frac{1}{5}, \frac{1}{6}, \frac{1}{7}, \frac{1}{8}$

   G $\frac{4}{7}, \frac{3}{5}, \frac{2}{3}, \frac{1}{4}$

   H $\frac{1}{8}, \frac{1}{7}, \frac{1}{6}, \frac{1}{5}$

   J $\frac{1}{4}, \frac{3}{5}, \frac{3}{5}, \frac{4}{7}$

3. **Keiko paid 0.28 of her yearly earnings in taxes. What fraction of her yearly earnings did she NOT pay in taxes?**

   A $3\frac{4}{7}$ **C** $\frac{18}{25}$

   B $\frac{17}{18}$ **D** $\frac{7}{25}$

4. **Which of these is equivalent to $\frac{4}{5}$?**

   F 0.4

   G 0.08

   H 40%

   J 80%

5. **Which of these is equivalent to $7\frac{9}{16}$?**

   A $7\frac{3}{4}$

   B $6\frac{16}{9}$

   C $6\frac{16}{25}$

   D $6\frac{25}{16}$

6. **Which point is at -2?**

   F P

   G Q

   H R

   J S

>GO ON>

7. Which list is composed of only prime numbers?

   A 2, 3, 4, 5

   B 11, 13, 15, 17

   C 9, 15, 21, 25

   D 7, 11, 13, 17

8. Which of the following shows the standard form for 5^4?

   F 9

   G 20

   H 50

   J 625

9. The minimum distance of Earth from the sun is about 91.4 million miles. Which of the following expresses this in scientific notation?

   A 9.14×10^6

   B 9.14×10^7

   C 9.14×10^8

   D 91.4×10^7

10. Which is the value of the underlined digit?

    153.0574

    F 5 tenths   H 5 thousandths

    G 5 hundreds   J 5 hundredths

11. Find the value of the expression $x(2y + 4)$ when x is equal to 3 and y is equal to -5.

    A -54

    B -26

    C -18

    D -3

12. Maria rakes leaves to earn extra money. She charges $6 per hour. Each time she rakes a yard, she donates $3 to the local animal shelter in her neighborhood. Which expression below describes the amount of money Maria has after she rakes one yard and then makes her donation? Let x = number of hours.

    F $6x - 3$

    G $6x + 3$

    H $6(x - 3)$

    J $3(x - 6)$

13. Which sentence describes the equation $4(x - 3) = 16$?

    A 3 more than 4 times a number is equal to 16.

    B 3 less than 4 times a number is equal to 16.

    C The product of 4 and 3 minus a number is equal to 16.

    D 4 times the difference of a number and 3 is equal to 16.

>GO ON>

14. Jane's word processing program is set up on a computer that has 34 megabytes of random access memory. If 22 megabytes are used by other programs, solve $x + 22 \leq 34$ to describe the number of megabytes of memory available for the word processing program. Which of the following graphs shows the solution set?

F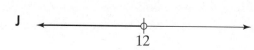
   12

G ←——————○——————→
          12

H ←——————●——————→
          12

J ←——————○——————→
          12

15. Solve for y: $3y - 2 = 8 + y$.

A $y = 5$

B $y = 4$

C $y = \frac{3}{2}$

D $y = 2.5$

16. Find the next two numbers in the sequence: 6, 24, 96, 384, . . .

F 1536, 6144

G 964, 3896

H 768, 1424

J 686, 1864

17. Barbara could not remember how much she was paying for using her cellular phone. She looked at her bill and saw that she paid a total of $12.88 for 56 minutes of air time. How much is she paying for each minute?

A 22 cents per minute

B 23 cents per minute

C 28 cents per minute

D 50 cents per minute

18. Complete the table for the equation $y = x + 2$.

x	y
−6	−4
−3	?
0	?
1	?
4	?

F −5, 2, 3, 5

G −1, 2, 3, 4

H −1, 2, 3, 6

J 1, 2, 3, 6

>GO ON>

19. The members of the Ecology Club want to order T-shirts. Each member gets to select his or her T-shirt from 5 colors, 4 patterns, 3 styles, and 3 sizes. How many different combinations of T-shirts are there?

A 40 combinations

B 60 combinations

C 90 combinations

D 180 combinations

20. In May, Anthony's Pastry Shop sold 83 chocolate cakes, 35 yellow cakes, 30 carrot cakes, and 12 orange cakes. Anthony expects to sell 20 cakes on Saturday. How many of these cakes can he expect to be chocolate?

F 20 chocolate cakes

G 15 chocolate cakes

H 10 chocolate cakes

J 5 chocolate cakes

21. Maxine, an environmentalist, caught 40 fish and found that 14 of them had high levels of mercury. Assuming this is proportional to the entire fish population of the lake, 2,500, predict how many fish in the lake have high levels of mercury.

A 875 fish

B 950 fish

C 1200 fish

D 8700 fish

22. What is the theoretical probability of flipping a head on a coin *and* rolling a 6 on a number cube?

F $\frac{1}{2}$

G $\frac{4}{9}$

H $\frac{1}{6}$

J $\frac{1}{12}$

23. The number of books read by 11 students during this past summer is displayed in the line plot below. Find the mean, median, and the mode of the data.

Books Read by Students

```
X         X   X
X   X   X   X
X   X   X   X
4   5   6   7
```
Number of Books

A Mean: 6; median: $5.\overline{54}$; modes: 4, 6, 7

B Mean: $5.\overline{54}$ median: 6; modes: 4, 6, 7

C Mean: $5.\overline{54}$; median: 6; mode: 5

D Mean: $5.\overline{54}$, median: 4, 6, 7; mode: 6

GO ON

Name _____ Class _____ Date _____

PS SAT 10 Practice Test

24. What is the approximate mean number of hours spent per week on leisure activities for teens?

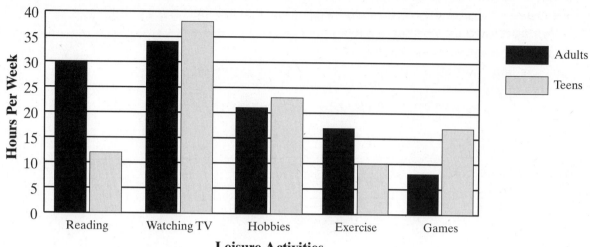

18 hours
F

20 hours
G

22 hours
H

24 hours
J

25. Which stem-and-leaf diagram shows the following data?
13, 15, 22, 24, 26, 26

A

Stem	Leaf
111	3 5 5
222	2 2 4 6 6

B

Stem	Leaf
1	3 5
2	2 4 6

C

Stem	Leaf
1	3 5
2	2 4 6 6

D

Stem	Leaf
111	3 5

26. Which statement is true for the scatterplot?

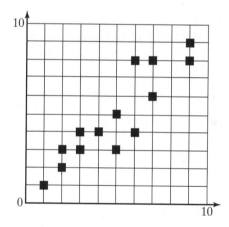

F The scatterplot shows a positive trend.

G The scatterplot shows a negative trend.

H The scatterplot shows no trend.

J The scatterplot shows a trend of no change.

27. Carol counted the number of people who came to her cafe at various hours throughout the afternoon. She made the following tally chart. Find the number of people who came to the cafe between 2:00 P.M. and 5:00 P.M.

Time	Number of People
1:00 – 2:00 P.M.	𝍸𝍸 𝍸𝍸 IIII
2:00 – 3:00 P.M.	𝍸𝍸 II
3:00 – 4:00 P.M.	𝍸𝍸 IIII
4:00 – 5:00 P.M.	𝍸𝍸 𝍸𝍸
5:00 – 6:00 P.M.	𝍸𝍸 𝍸𝍸 𝍸𝍸 I

A 22 people

B 26 people

C 38 people

D 42 people

28. Which of the following are a radius and a diameter of circle *0*?

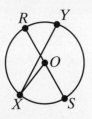

F Radius *RS* and diameter *OX*

G Radius *OX* and diameter *XY*

H Radius *OX* and diameter *RS*

J Radius *XY* and diameter *OX*

29. Which shape has no parallel line segments?

A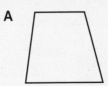

B

C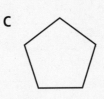

D

GO ON

PS SAT 10 Practice Test

30. How many faces does this figure have?

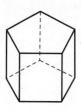

F 2 faces

G 5 faces

H 7 faces

J 8 faces

31. Compute the area of the figure below.

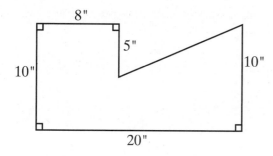

A 165 in.^{2} **C** 180 in.^{2}

B 170 in.^{2} **D** 230 in.^{2}

32. Margie wants to cover the top of a round table with contact paper. If the diameter of the table is 36 inches, how much contact paper will she need?
Use $A = \pi r^2$. Use $\pi = 3.14$.

F 56.52 in.^{2}

G 113.04 in.^{2}

H 1017.36 in.^{2}

J 4069.44 in.^{2}

33. The radius of a circle is 3 meters. What is the circumference?
Use $C = 2\pi r$. Use $\pi = 3.14$.

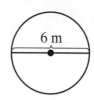

6 m

A 18.84 m

B 37.68 m

C 78.94 m

D 113.04 m

GO ON

34. Find the volume of the prism.

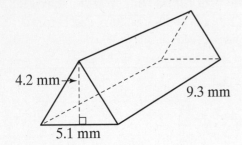

4.2 mm
9.3 mm
5.1 mm

F 308.5 mm³

G 199.206 mm³

H 180 mm³

J 99.603 mm³

35. If you slide the triangle down three units, what are the coordinates of the vertices of triangle *PQR*?

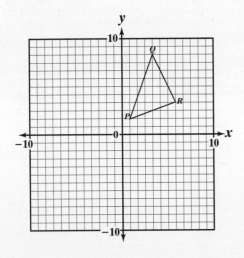

A $P(-2, 2), Q(1, 8), R(4, 4)$

B $P(1, -1), Q(4, 5), R(7, 1)$

C $P(1, 5), Q(4, 11), R(7, 7)$

D $P(4, 2), Q(7, 8), R(10, 4)$

36. Which illustration shows the figure below after a 270° counterclockwise rotation?

F

G

H

J

37. The figures below are similar. Find the length *m*.

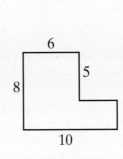

6
5
8
10

9
m
12
15

A $m = 6$

B $m = 7.5$

C $m = 8$

D $m = 10$

GO ON

Name _____ Class _____ Date _____

38. Which of these angles has a measure closest to 90°?

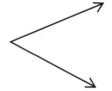

F

G

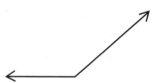

H

J

39. Sara filled a container by pouring six 8-ounce glasses of water into it. What is the capacity of Sara's container in quarts?

A 1.5 quarts

B 15 quarts

C 32 quarts

D 48 quarts

40. Use a centimeter ruler. Find the area of the rectangle.

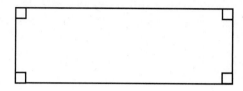

F 32 cm^2

G 24 cm^2

H 16 cm^2

J 12 cm^2

41. This scale drawing shows the floor plan for Jennifer's studio apartment. The scale is 3 in. = 5 ft. What are the actual dimensions in feet?

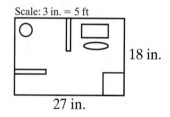

Scale: 3 in. = 5 ft

18 in.

27 in.

A 24 ft by 36 ft

B 30 ft by 45 ft

C 36 ft by 90 ft

D 54 ft by 135 ft

GO ON

42. Maria bought a blouse for $19.95, a skirt for $27.95, and two pairs of pants for $21.95 each. About how much did she spend?

F $100.00

G $90.00

H $80.00

J $70.00

43. Doug wants to enclose his yard with a fence. The figure below shows the shape and dimensions of Doug's yard. Estimate how much fencing he needs around the perimeter of his yard.

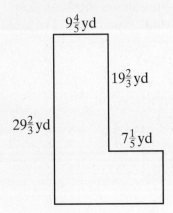

A About 74 yd

B About 84 yd

C About 94 yd

D About 104 yd

44. Sara has collected 3985 stamps so far. She has 787 stamps from countries other than the United States. What percent of the stamps are from countries other than the United States?

F 200%

G 50%

H 30%

J 20%

45. Estimate the sum of these measures: 1 hour 52 minutes, 2 hours 6 minutes, 2 hours 3 minutes, 1 hour 58 minutes.

A About 6 hours

B About 7 hours

C About 8 hours

D About 9 hours

46. Nola makes wreaths for a craft fair. She uses 46 feet of ribbon to make 15 wreaths. About how much ribbon would she need to make 100 wreaths?

F 460 ft

G 300 ft

H 150 ft

J 75 ft

GO ON

PS SAT 10 Practice Test

47. **A Tyrannosaurus rex was about 40 ft long from head to tail. Ralph wants to make a scale drawing that fits on a sheet of paper that measures $8\frac{1}{2}$ inches by 11 inches. Which is a reasonable scale for his drawing?**

A 1 inch represents 1 ft

B $\frac{1}{4}$ inch represents 1 ft

C $\frac{1}{2}$ inch represents 1 ft

D 1 inch represents 40 ft

48. **Tickets to a musical cost $38.50 for adults and $22.75 for children. On Friday, 643 tickets were sold. What information do you need to find out how much money was collected on Friday?**

F The price of a ticket

G The number of tickets sold on Thursday

H The number of senior citizens who attended the musical

J The number of adult tickets sold on Friday

49. **Joe, Donna, and Rick are taxi drivers several evenings a week. Joe drives every third evening, Donna drives every other evening, and Rick drives every fourth evening. How often will all three drive on the same evening?**

A Every 6 evenings

B Every 9 evenings

C Every 12 evenings

D Every 24 evenings

50. **Keith, Frank, and Sandy volunteered to put books from a table back on the shelves at the library. Keith took $\frac{1}{3}$ of the total number of books, Frank took $\frac{1}{2}$ of what was left, and Sandy took the remaining 10 books. How many books were on the table to start with?**

F 45 books

G 30 books

H 15 books

J 10 books

GO ON

51. Stan, Rhonda, and Tammy have favorite pastimes of watching movies, reading books, and solving puzzles, though not necessarily in that order. Stan hates puzzles. Rhonda plays golf with the person who likes to read books but not the person who likes to solve puzzles. Match each person with his or her favorite pastime.

A Stan likes books. Rhonda likes puzzles, and Tammy likes movies.

B Stan likes movies, Rhonda likes books, and Tammy likes puzzles.

C Stan likes puzzles. Rhonda likes movies, and Tammy likes books.

D Stan likes books, Rhonda likes movies, and Tammy likes puzzles.

52. Darla is sewing ribbon together in the shape of a pentagon. The length of the side of each pentagon is 1 inch. What is the total length of ribbon needed for 12 pentagons?

F 12 in.

G 24 in.

H 60 in.

J 72 in.

SAT 10 Practice Test

• •

Mathematics: Procedures

Find each answer. Then mark the space on your answer sheet. If a correct answer is not here, mark the space for NH.

1. $5.1 + 1.35 + 12.02 =$

   A 14.38   D 19.07

   B 15.47   E NH

   C 18.47

2. $\frac{5}{9} - \frac{2}{3} =$

   F $-\frac{1}{9}$ J $\frac{7}{12}$

   G $\frac{2}{18}$ K NH

   H $\frac{1}{3}$

3. 5.24
    $\times\ 2.5$

   A 13.1   D 13,100

   B 131   E NH

   C 1310

4. $34 \div \frac{2}{3} =$

   F 17   J $51\frac{2}{3}$

   G $17\frac{2}{3}$ K NH

   H $22\frac{2}{3}$

5. $8\frac{2}{9}$
   $+\ 3\frac{8}{9}$

   A $13\frac{1}{9}$ D $11\frac{1}{9}$

   B $12\frac{2}{9}$ E NH

   C $12\frac{1}{9}$

6. $(-3) \times (-3) \times (-3) =$

   F -27 J $\frac{10}{27}$

   G -9 K NH

   H 27

7. $16.24 \div 0.8 =$

   A 203   D 0.203

   B 20.3   E NH

   C 2.03

8. $-35 + 7 + (-19) + (-7) =$

   F 68

   G 54

   H -54

   J -68

   K NH

GO ON →

SAT 10 Practice Test

9. Carlos wants to build a single-rail fence around his property that has a perimeter of 195 ft. How many 8-ft boards would he need?

   A 20 boards   **D** 30 boards

   B 23 boards   **E** NH

   C 25 boards

10. Pablo is a marathon runner. He burns up 120 calories every ten minutes of a race. How many calories does he burn up in the first 24 minutes of a race?

   F 2880 calories   **J** 244 calories

   G 360 calories   **K** NH

   H 288 calories

11. What is the perimeter of the triangular path?

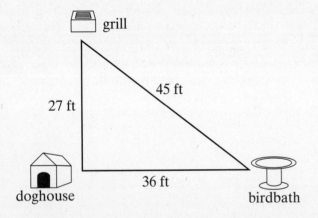

   A 97 ft

   B 98 ft

   C 99 ft

   D 107 ft

   E NH

12. An 18-ounce box of cereal sells for $2.88. What is the unit cost of the cereal?

   F $0.16   **J** $3.19

   G $0.18   **K** NH

   H $2.99

13. If $\frac{9}{28}$ of the students at Willard High School participate in after-school sports activities, what fraction of the students do not participate in after-school sports activities?

   A $\frac{3}{4}$ **D** $\frac{1}{3}$

   B $\frac{19}{28}$ **E** NH

   C $\frac{2}{7}$

14. Tony jogs $4\frac{2}{5}$ miles from the gym to his home daily. If he takes a water break after $2\frac{1}{4}$ miles, how much farther does he have to jog to get home?

   F $2\frac{3}{20}$ miles   **J** $1\frac{4}{5}$ miles

   G $2\frac{2}{5}$ miles   **K** NH

   H $2\frac{3}{4}$ miles

15. Carla figures she spends 21% of her income on food. Which fraction is a good estimate for 21%?

   A $\frac{1}{10}$ **D** $\frac{1}{2}$

   B $\frac{1}{5}$ **E** NH

   C $\frac{1}{3}$

Name _____ Class _____ Date _____

SAT 10 Practice Test

16. Pears are $1.98 a pound. How much do 3.5 pounds of pears cost?

    F $69.30   **J** $6.83

    G $15.84   **K** NH

    H $6.93

17. Jennie worked 52 hours last week and was paid $429. How much was she paid per hour?

    A $8.25   **D** $9.45

    B $8.50   **E** NH

    C $9.00

18. Tyler uses $32\frac{1}{2}$ gallons of water in one week to prepare dinner and do dishes. Of that amount, about $\frac{1}{4}$ is bottled water. How much of the total is bottled water?

    F $3\frac{1}{2}$ gal   **J** $32\frac{1}{4}$ gal

    G $8\frac{1}{8}$ gal   **K** NH

    H $16\frac{1}{2}$ gal

19. Arlene has a piece of cloth that is $7\frac{1}{8}$ yards long. She cuts a piece that is $4\frac{3}{4}$ yards long to make a skirt. How much cloth is left?

    A $3\frac{1}{8}$ yd   **D** $1\frac{2}{3}$ yd

    B $2\frac{3}{8}$ yd   **E** NH

    C $2\frac{1}{4}$ yd

20. Use the formula $d = rt$ to find the distance traveled by a train at a rate of 55 mph for $3\frac{1}{2}$ hours.

    F $192\frac{1}{2}$ miles   **J** $58\frac{1}{2}$ miles

    G $190\frac{1}{2}$ miles   **K** NH

    H $168\frac{1}{2}$ miles

21. One recipe makes $8\frac{1}{2}$ cups of potato salad. If one serving is $\frac{1}{2}$ cup, how many servings does the recipe make?

    A 17 servings   **D** 4 servings

    B 16 servings   **E** NH

    C $4\frac{1}{4}$ servings

22. Mr. Harris made $837.37 selling hot dogs at a concert. His expenses were 22% of the amount he made. How much did he earn after expenses?

    F $563.00   **J** $800.00

    G $653.15   **K** NH

    H $783.35

GO ON

23. Tyler has 240 cards in a collection. Of all of the cards, $\frac{1}{3}$ are baseball cards, $\frac{1}{6}$ are basketball cards, and $\frac{1}{4}$ are football cards. The rest are hockey cards. How many of the cards are hockey cards?

A 20 cards **D** 80 cards

B 40 cards **E** NH

C 60 cards

24. Kenny is going to purchase a parakeet and cage for $45. He will spend $7 per month on food for his new parakeet. How much money will Kenny need to obtain a parakeet and keep it for one year?

F $129 **J** $39

G $119 **K** NH

H $84

25. Jake is using two tables for a work bench. The first table is 4 ft by 3 ft. The second table is 5 ft by 3 ft. If he puts the two tables next to each other, what is the area of his work bench?

A 25 ft^2 **D** 180 ft^2

B 32 ft^2 **E** NH

C 45 ft^2

26. There are 120 students involved in the school play. If 72 of the students are girls, what percent are girls?

F 72% **J** 6%

G 60% **K** NH

H 40%

27. What is 7.368 rounded to the nearest tenth?

A 7.4 **D** 7.3

B 7.37 **E** NH

C 7.36

28. In-line skates regularly sell for $49.99 at Jimmy's Sports Store. What is the price after a discount of 25%?

F $53.00 **J** $12.90

G $37.49 **K** NH

H $25.00

29. What is the mean temperature for the four days?

Mon.	Tues.	Wed.	Thurs.
56.3°F	58.1°F	61.4°F	63.4°F

A 58.1°F **D** 87.80°F

B 56.3°F **E** NH

C 54.6°F

30. On his first flight, John Glenn spent 4.923 hours in orbit. What is this rounded to the nearest tenth?

F 5.0 **J** 4.9

G 4.93 **K** NH

H 4.92

ITBS Practice Test

• •

Read each question and choose the best answer. Then mark the space on the answer sheet for the answer you have chosen.

1. Which of the following percents are in order from greatest to least?

   A 98%, 98.05%, 98.50%, 98.005%

   B 98.50%, 98.05%, 98.005%, 98%

   C 98.50%, 98.005%, 98.05%, 98%

   D 98%, 98.50%, 98.05%, 98.005%

2. $693 + 418 =$

   F 1111

   G 1101

   H 1011

   J 1001

3. Charlotte measured the height of a plant every week as part of an assignment for science class. Last week the plant was 11.2 centimeters high, and this week the plant is 14.1 centimeters high. How much did the plant grow?

   A 2.1 cm

   B 2.9 cm

   C 3.1 cm

   D Not Here

4. Which of the following number sentences is true?

   F $\frac{5}{8} > \frac{3}{4}$

   G $\frac{3}{9} < \frac{1}{3}$

   H $\frac{5}{6} > \frac{2}{3}$

   J $\frac{3}{5} < \frac{4}{10}$

5. Carmen bought 6 items at the grocery store that ranged in price from $0.89 to $3.29. Which amount of money guarantees that she can afford the items? Assume there is no tax.

   A $4.18

   B $6.00

   C $12.00

   D $20.00

▷GO ON▷

• •

ITBS Practice Test

6. Simplify $24 \div (8 - 2) + 3 \cdot 4$.

   F 13

   G 16

   H 18

   J 26

7. The graph shows the percentages of apartment residents in each age category. Which 2 age groups make up more than $\frac{1}{3}$ of all apartment residents?

AGE OF APARTMENT RESIDENTS

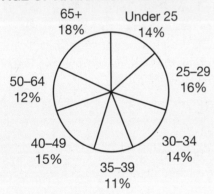

   A 25–29 and 65+

   B Under 25 and 25–29

   C 50–64 and 65+

   D 30–34 and 35–39

8. What is the greatest prime factor of 273?

   F 7

   G 13

   H 39

   J 91

9. The table below shows the results of the mayor election in a town.

Mayor Election Results

Candidate	Fraction of Votes
Morales	$\frac{7}{20}$
Werner	$\frac{2}{5}$
Lee	$\frac{1}{10}$
Clayton	$\frac{3}{20}$

What fraction of the votes were for Werner or Clayton?

   A $\frac{1}{20}$

   B $\frac{1}{2}$

   C $\frac{11}{20}$

   D $\frac{7}{10}$

10. A room is to be carpeted with carpet that costs $15.99 per square yard. If the room is square and has an area of 40 square yards, what is the approximate length of the room?

   F 6.3 yd

   G 8.9 yd

   H 12.8 yd

   J 20 yd

GO ON

ITBS Practice Test

11. If Mr. McNamara drives at an average speed of 53 miles per hour, which is the closest estimate of the distance he can travel in 6.5 hours?

   A 300 mi

   B 350 mi

   C 360 mi

   D 420 mi

12. Which of these sets of numbers has elements that are all divisible by 3?

   F {12, 21, 27, 33}

   G {13, 23, 33, 43}

   H {21, 27, 19, 63}

   J {24, 9, 27, 83}

13. What is the rule for this number sequence?

   2, 7, 22, 67, 202

   A Multiply by 3, then subtract 1

   B Multiply by 2, then add 3

   C Multiply by 3, then add 1

   D Multiply by 2, then subtract 1

14. Simplify the expression 6^4.

   F 24

   G 72

   H 216

   J 1,296

15. Which equation has a solution of 0.6?

   A $3x - 0.5 = 2.0$

   B $4x - 0.5 = 1.9$

   C $1.3 + 2x = -1.1$

   D $1.2 + 2x = 3.0$

16. Which group of fractions is in order from greatest to least?

   F $-\frac{2}{3}, -\frac{7}{9}, -\frac{3}{4}, -\frac{5}{6}$

   G $-\frac{5}{6}, -\frac{3}{4}, -\frac{7}{9}, -\frac{2}{3}$

   H $-\frac{3}{4}, -\frac{2}{3}, -\frac{7}{9}, -\frac{5}{6}$

   J $-\frac{2}{3}, -\frac{3}{4}, -\frac{7}{9}, -\frac{5}{6}$

GO ON

ITBS Practice Test

17. The student council needs to buy 45 table decorations for the spring dance. Each table decoration costs $3.75. What is the total cost for the decorations?

A $48.75

B $146.25

C $168.75

D $180.00

18. Find the difference.

$$\frac{7}{9} - \frac{2}{3}$$

F $\frac{1}{9}$

G $\frac{1}{3}$

H $\frac{5}{9}$

J $\frac{5}{6}$

19.
$$\begin{array}{r} 59 \\ \times\ 37 \\ \hline \end{array}$$

A 413

B 2183

C 1923

D 590

20. 85% of 32 =

F 272

G 37.6

H 27.2

J 0.272

21. A number cube and a spinner are used in a game. The spinner has an equal chance of landing on any one of 5 colors: red, blue, green, yellow, orange. The number cube has numbers 1 through 6 on its faces. What is the probability of rolling a 6 and spinning the color red?

A $\frac{1}{30}$

B $\frac{1}{6}$

C $\frac{1}{5}$

D $\frac{11}{30}$

22. Ryan volunteered to spend 80 hours working at a nature center. He has already worked for 10 hours and plans to work 3.5 hours each week. Solve the equation $10 + 3.5w = 80$ to find the number of weeks (w) it will take Ryan to complete his hours.

F 10

G 12

H 20

J 22

GO ON

Name_____ Class_____ Date_____

ITBS Practice Test

23. $385 \div 22 =$

    A 17 R11

    B 17 R9

    C 18

    D 17 R1

24. Drew made a score of 29 out of 35 points on a recent assignment. About what percentage score did he receive?

    F 80%   **H** 60%

    G 70%   **J** 29%

25. Which of these nets cannot be folded to make a cube?

    A
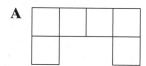

    B
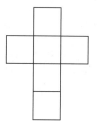

    C
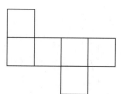

    D
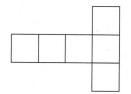

26. During swim practice Benita swam $\frac{5}{8}$ mile and Nadia swam $\frac{7}{10}$ mile. How much farther did Nadia swim than Benita?

    F $\frac{1}{40}$ mi

    G $\frac{1}{20}$ mi

    H $\frac{3}{40}$ mi

    J $\frac{3}{20}$ mi

27. $\frac{2}{9} \times 9 =$

    A $18\frac{1}{9}$

    B 2

    C $2\frac{1}{2}$

    D $1\frac{2}{9}$

28. The table below shows the cost C for buying x pounds of tomatoes. Which equation represents the cost C?

x = pounds	1	2	3	4
C = cost (in dollars)	0.90	1.80	2.70	3.60

    F $C = 0.90x + 1$

    G $C = 0.90x$

    H $x = 0.90C$

    J $C = x + 0.90$

GO ON

29. A middle school soccer team is choosing a new uniform. The team can choose from 5 types of jerseys and 4 types of shorts. How many different combinations of shirts and shorts can the team choose?

   A 9

   B 15

   C 18

   D 20

30. Which expression would best help you estimate 49% of 377?

   F 49% of 300

   G 49% of 350

   H 50% of 350

   J 50% of 380

31. $45.9 + 6.78 =$

   A 1137

   B 51.28

   C 52.68

   D 11.37

32. These temperature readings were taken at 1:00 P.M. each day for a week.

   77°F, 77°F, 69°F, 66°F, 67°F, 70°F, 71°F

What is the mean temperature for the week?

   F 70°F

   G 71°F

   H 74°F

   J 77°F

33. 5% of $50 =

   A $25

   B $20

   C $2

   D $2.50

ITBS Practice Test

34. The graph shows the number of meals, on average, people in the United States eat at restaurants each year.

ANNUAL RESTAURANT PURCHASES (PER PERSON)

Based on the graph, which is the best estimate of the average number of meals eaten out, per person, in 1986?

F 131

G 123

H 118

J 112

35. $4.3 \times 1.5 =$

A 6.45

B 64.5

C 5.8

D 2.58

36. Solve for w.

$$w - 3 = 28$$

F 211

G 25

H $2\frac{2}{3}$

J 31

37. The table shows the number of miles driven by a race car after a given number of laps.

Number of laps	1	2	3	4	5
Number of miles driven	2.6	5.2	7.8	10.4	13.0

Which equation represents the number of miles M to the number of laps L?

A $M = L + 2.6$

B $M = L \div 2.6$

C $M = 2.6L$

D Not Here

GO ON

ITBS Practice Test

38. Solve for x.

$$-3x + 5 = -1$$

   F $-1\frac{1}{3}$

   G -2

   H 2

   J -6

39. $\frac{21}{48} \times \frac{8}{45} =$

   A $\frac{1}{10}$

   B $\frac{7}{90}$

   C $\frac{1}{15}$

   D $\frac{7}{8}$

40. The box in which a refrigerator is shipped is 33 inches wide, 30 inches long, and 67 inches high. What is the volume of this box?

   F 130 in.^{3}

   G 5,211 in.^{3}

   H 10,422 in.^{3}

   J 66,330 in.^{3}

TerraNova Practice Test

Part 1

Read each question and choose the best answer. Then mark the space on the answer sheet for the answer you have chosen.

1 $6\overline{)0.438}$

   A 0.073

   B 0.73

   C 73

   D 730

   E None of these

2 $15 - 3^2 =$

   F 144

   G 9

   H 7

   J -1

   K None of these

3 $-4(5 - 9) =$

   A -29

   B -16

   C 16

   D 29

   E None of these

4 Which of these is another way to write the following expression?
$-4 \times -4 \times -4 \times -4 \times -4$

   F 4^{-5}

   G 4^5

   H $(-4)^{-5}$

   J $(-4)^5$

   K None of these

5 Katy left a 15% tip for a restaurant bill of $25. How much was the tip?

   A $2.00

   B $3.00

   C $3.75

   D $4.50

   E None of these

6 How much flooring is needed to cover a floor that measures 9 feet by 14 feet?

   F 252 ft^2

   G 126 ft^2

   H 46 ft^2

   J 23 ft

   K None of these

GO ON

TerraNova Practice Test

7 Evaluate x^3 for $x = -3$.

A -9

B 9

C -27

D 27

8 Solve. $x + 0.78 = 1.32$

F $x = 2.1$

G $x = 0.54$

H $x = 0.46$

J $x = 9.12$

9 The Drama Club budgeted $952 for a class trip to a musical comedy. Each person's ticket will cost $32.50. What is the greatest number of people that can attend the musical comedy?

A 20 people

B 25 people

C 29 people

D 32 people

10 Mount Gray has an altitude of 600 feet. If the base of the slope where Sam is standing is 1,000 feet from the peak, how far is Sam from the pipe?

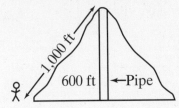

F 1,600 ft

G 1,200 ft

H 800 ft

J 600 ft

11 Which is the greatest common factor of 18, 24, and 36?

A 12

B 6

C 1

D 3

12 How many decimal places will be in this product?
0.007×0.9

F 2 places

G 1 place

H 4 places

J 6 places

TerraNova Practice Test

Part 2

13 Which of these is equivalent to $7\frac{9}{16}$?

A $6\frac{16}{9}$ C $6\frac{25}{16}$

B $7\frac{3}{4}$ D $6\frac{16}{25}$

14 Find the fraction, decimal, percent, or ratio that does NOT describe how much of the figure is shaded.

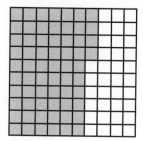

F $16:25$ H 64%

G 0.64 J $\frac{100}{64}$

15 Which addition problem is represented by the model?

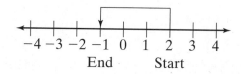

$$\begin{array}{c} \text{End} \qquad\qquad \text{Start} \end{array}$$

A $-3 + 2 = -1$

B $2 + -3 = -1$

C $-3 + 2 = 1$

D $2 + -3 = 1$

16 Which picture shows the ratio of circles to triangles as $3:2$?

F ○ ○ △ △ △

G ○ △ ○ △ ○

H △ ○ △ ○ △

J ○ △ △ ○ △

17 Which decimal is equivalent to $-\frac{5}{8}$?

A -1.375

B 1.375

C -0.625

D 0.625

18 Keiko found that 0.28 of her yearly earnings go for taxes. What fraction of her yearly earnings do NOT go for taxes?

F $3\frac{4}{7}$

G $1\frac{7}{18}$

H $\frac{18}{25}$

J $\frac{7}{25}$

GO ON

TerraNova Practice Test

19 Which of these is the perimeter of the figure below?

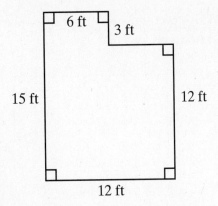

A 60 ft   **C** 48 ft

B 54 ft   **D** 45 ft

20 Solve. $2x + 8 > 32$

F $x > 20$ **H** $x > 24$

G $x > 12$ **J** $x > 10$

21 Find the area of the triangle after a dilation using the given scale factor. Scale factor = 1.5

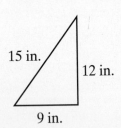

A 243 in.²

B 121.5 in.²

C 81 in.²

D 54 in.

22 Find the volume of the cone. Use 3.14 for π.

F 56.52 cm³

G 28.26 cm³

H 18.84 cm³

J 9.42 cm³

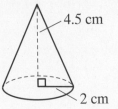

23 $\overleftrightarrow{AB} \parallel \overleftrightarrow{CD}$. Find the measure of $\angle CFE$.

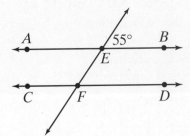

A 180°

B 125°

C 55°

D 45°

24 Jeanne ran for $\frac{1}{2}$ hour at a speed of 5 miles per hour. Use the formula $d = rt$ to find how far she ran. (d = distance, r = rate, t = time)

F 1 mi

G $2\frac{1}{2}$ mi

H 5 mi

J 10 mi

GO ON

TerraNova Practice Test

25 Louis wants to find the capacity of a dropper used for a single dose of medicine for his cat. What unit of measure should he use?

A millimeter

B milliliter

C milligram

D kilogram

26 If the sequence in the pattern continues, how many dots would there be in the ninth set of dots?

set 1   set 2   set 3   set 4

F 55

G 45

H 65

J 90

27 What is a possible rule for the input and output shown?

Input	−3	−2	−1	0
Output	−9	−6	−3	0

A Multiply by −3

B Multiply by 3

C Divide by 3

D Divide by −3

28 Given the function rule $y = 3x + 2$, find the missing value.

Input (x)	−1	0	1	2
Output (y)	−1	2	5	?

F 4

G 6

H 8

J 10

29 Which statement is not true for the table below?

Input (x)	−2	−1	0	−1	−2
Output (y)	6	3	0	−3	−6

A It represents a function.

B It does not represent a function.

C Some input values have more than one output value.

D The graph of this relationship would not be a line.

>GO ON

TerraNova Practice Test

30 A zoo has six types of rare birds. The populations of each type are 15, 22, 14, 21, 25, and 21. Which stem-and-leaf plot shows this data?

F

Stem	Leaf
1	4 5 5
2	1 1 2

G

Stem	Leaf
1	4 5
2	1 2 5

H

Stem	Leaf
1	2 4 5
2	1 2 5

J

Stem	Leaf
1	4 5
2	1 1 2 5

31 Which expression is equivalent to $5(n + 8)$?

A $(5 + n)8$

B $5n + 40$

C $n + 13$

D $5n + 8$

32 The Camera Club charges a flat fee of $5.25 plus $4 per hour for renting a video camera. Which equation relates the cost (c) of renting the camera to the number of hours (h) the camera is used?

F $h = 5.25c + 4$

G $c = 5.25h + 4$

H $h = 4c + 5.25$

J $c = 4h + 5.25$

33 Dan patrolled the same parking zone over and over all day. It took him 30 minutes to complete one round. Which expression would give the number of rounds Dan would complete in h hours?

A $2h$

B $30h$

C $\dfrac{h}{2}$

D $\dfrac{h}{30}$

>GO ON>

TerraNova Practice Test

34 The graph of a linear equation is shown below. Which ordered pair is a solution of that linear equation?

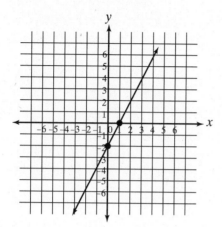

F $(-2, 0)$ H $(1, 0)$

G $(0, 2)$ J $(2, 0)$

35 Which is the graph of the inequality $x < 4$?

A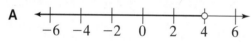

B
```
  -6  -4  -2   0   2   4   6
```

C
```
  -6  -4  -2   0   2   4   6
```

D
```
  -6  -4  -2   0   2   4   6
```

36 At a horse show, the riders from one club scored 65, 48, 57, 70, 62, 58, and 53. What is the median score?

F 48

G 59

H 58

J 70

37 The chart below shows how many of each flavor of candy is in a brown paper bag. If you took a candy from the bag without looking, what is the probability that the candy would be strawberry flavored?

Flavor of Candy	Number of Each
Vanilla	9
Strawberry	12
Chocolate	24
Mocha	15

A 12

B $\frac{9}{60}$

C $\frac{12}{30}$

D $\frac{1}{5}$

GO ON

TerraNova Practice Test

Use the bar graph below to answer questions 38–40.
Kayla sells handwoven items at fairs during the 6-month season from
April to September. The graph below shows her sales for last season.

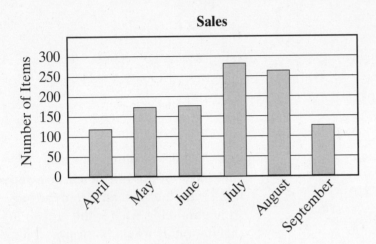

Sales

38 **Each year Kayla uses her sales graph to plan for the season coming up. During which months can Kayla expect to be the busiest this season?**

F   During the months of July and August

G   During the months of April and September

H   During the months of June and August

J   During the months of May and June

39 **What conclusion can you draw about probable attendance at the fairs during various months?**

A   Attendance is probably the least in April and May.

B   Attendance is probably the least in June and July.

C   Attendance is probably the least in April and September.

D   Attendance is probably the least in August and September.

40 **Between which two months did sales increase the most?**

F   Between April and May

G   Between May and June

H   Between June and July

J   Between August and September

Name_____ Class_____ Date_____

TerraNova Practice Test

41 An event has a probability of 1. What can you say about that event?

   A It is an impossible event.

   B It is an event that will happen occasionally.

   C It is a certain event.

   D It is an event that will happen often.

42 A test run at the Sunlight flash bulb factory found that 25 bulbs out of 625 bulbs were defective. Which is the best prediction of how many bulbs out of 5,000 would be defective?

   F 25 bulbs

   G 200 bulbs

   H 20 bulbs

   J 400 bulbs

43 Which of these lists includes all possible outcomes for drawing a marble from a bag with 2 red, 3 green, and 2 blue marbles?

   A R, G, B

   B R, G, G, B

   C R, R, G, G, G, B, B

   D R, R, G, G, G, B, B, B

44 What is the measure of the complement of $\angle CAB$?

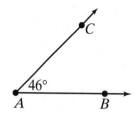

   F 44°   **H** 134°

   G 34°   **J** 90°

45 A triangle has been translated 5.5 units to the left and 2 units down. Find the coordinates of points *A* and *B* on the translation.

   A $A(-4.5, 0)$ and $B(-2.5, 3)$

   B $A(-4, 0)$ and $B(-2, 3)$

   C $A(-5.5, 0)$ and $B(0, 2)$

   D $A(-5, 0)$ and $B(-1, 2)$

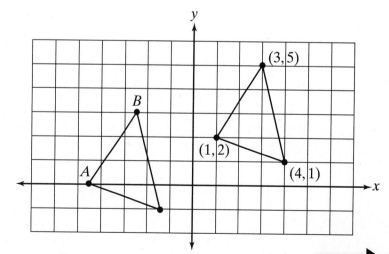

TerraNova Practice Test

46 A circular garden has an area of 36 square feet. Which is the best approximation for the radius of the garden? Use 3.14 for π.

F 11.46 ft

G 6 ft

H 4.34 ft

J 3.39 ft

47 The two triangles are similar. Find *x*.

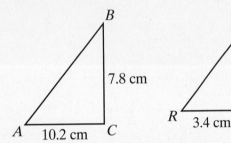

A 2.6 cm

B 3.2 cm

C 3.9 cm

D 4.45 cm

48 The slopes of two lines are given. Which represent parallel lines?

F $\frac{9}{3}$ and $\frac{3}{9}$

G 5 and $\frac{1}{5}$

H $\frac{3}{9}$ and $-\frac{3}{9}$

J $\frac{10}{5}$ and $\frac{8}{4}$

49 An architect is planning a path around the outside of an odd-shaped cabin. Use the floor plan to find the perimeter around the cabin. (Hint: First find the value of *y*.)

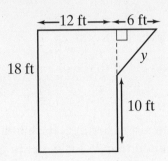

A 66 ft   C 76 ft

B 68 ft   D 80 ft

50 The Earth's diameter is approximately 7,961 miles. Find the approximate circumference of the Earth. Use 3.14 for π.

F 50,000 mi   H 5,500 mi

G 25,000 mi   J 2,536 mi

51 Tanya sees a bird on top of a light pole that is 27 feet tall. If she is 50 feet from the light pole, approximately how far is she from the bird?

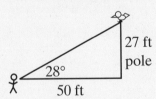

A 24 ft   C 94 ft

B 57 ft   D 250 ft

GO ON

TerraNova Practice Test

52 A lens casts an image of a 15-foot tree onto a sheet of paper. The image is 8 inches from the lens, and the lens is 12 feet from the tree. Find the height of the image.

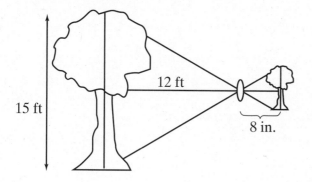

F 10 in.

G 6 in.

H 4 in.

J 12 in.

53 Find the volume of the figure after a dilation using the given scale factor.
Scale factor = 0.2

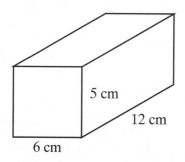

A 2.88 cm³

B 14.4 cm³

C 23.04 cm³

D 72 cm³

54 Which is the best estimate of 34% of 898?

F 300

G 360

H 400

J 450

55 Find three hundred twenty-four hundred-thousandths expressed in scientific notation.

A 3.24×10^{-5}

B 32.4×10^{-4}

C 3.24×10^{-3}

D 32.4×10^{-2}

56 The front of a tent is an isosceles triangle with a base of 6 feet and a height of 4 feet. The length of the tent is 8 feet. What is the volume of the tent?

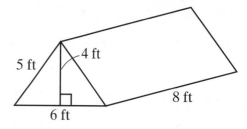

F 48 ft³

G 96 ft³

H 192 ft³

J 200 ft³

STOP

TerraNova Practice Test

Part 3

1   **120 is 16% of what number?**

   A   750

   B   630

   C   450

   D   230

   E   None of these

2   **12.56 − 1.2 =**

   F   12.44

   G   0.56

   H   11.36

   J   15.072

   K   None of these

3   **18 + 6 ÷ 3 − 1 =**

   A   7

   B   12

   C   18

   D   19

   E   None of these

4   **54 + (−23) =**

   F   −87

   G   −43

   H   31

   J   72

   K   None of these

5   **−46 − 82 =**

   A   468

   B   −108

   C   −126

   D   −148

   E   None of these

6 $\frac{4}{5} + \frac{6}{5} =$

   F   2

   G   1

   H $\frac{10}{25}$

   J $\frac{24}{25}$

   K   None of these

GO ON

TerraNova Practice Test

7 $\frac{9}{10} - \frac{6}{8} =$

A $\frac{3}{2}$

B $\frac{6}{20}$

C $\frac{3}{20}$

D $\frac{3}{40}$

E None of these

8 $\frac{4}{9} \times \frac{3}{8} =$

F $\frac{7}{72}$

G $\frac{1}{6}$

H $\frac{27}{32}$

J $\frac{32}{27}$

K None of these

9 $\frac{2}{3} \div \frac{5}{6} =$

A $\frac{5}{4}$

B $\frac{4}{5}$

C $\frac{1}{5}$

D $\frac{5}{9}$

E None of these

10 Solve for x. $-3x - 15 = -150$

F -45

G 45

H -18

J 12

K None of these

11 Simplify. $3x^2 + 2x - x^2 + 3x - 1$

A $3x^2 + 5x - 1$

B $3(x^2 - x) - 1$

C $7x^2 - 1$

D $2x^2 + 5x - 1$

E None of these

12 $\frac{-28}{14} =$

F $-\frac{1}{2}$

G $\frac{1}{2}$

H -2

J 2

K None of these

GO ON

TerraNova Practice Test

13 5% of 120 is what number?

A 0.6

B 6

C 60

D 600

E None of these

14 $-12 + 6 \div 3 + (-2) =$

F 0

G -3

H -4

J -12

K None of these

15 What percent of 25 is 10?

A 4%

B 25%

C 2.5%

D 40%

E None of these

16 $2^3 + 3^2 =$

F 12

G 13

H 17

J 25

K None of these

17 $2.05 \div 0.5 =$

A 0.041

B 4.1

C 41

D 0.41

E None of these

18 35% of what number is 70?

F 24.5

G 200

H 20

J 50

K None of these

19 $2(8 - 6)^2 \div 8 =$

A 2

B 7

C 1

D $36\frac{1}{2}$

E None of these

20 $-1 + (6 + 2) \div -2 =$

F 3

G 4

H -5

J 6

K None of these

Name _____ Class _____ Date _____

Screening Test Report

Mathematics Concepts	Test Item(s)	Proficient? Yes or No
Number Properties and Operations		
Identify the place value and actual value of digits in whole numbers.	1	
Connect model, word, or number using various models and representations for whole numbers, fractions, and decimals.	2	
Order or compare whole numbers, decimals, or fractions.	3	
Add and subtract whole numbers.	4, 5, 6	
Add and subtract fractions with unlike denominators.	7, 8	
Add and subtract decimals through thousandths.	9, 10	
Multiply and divide whole numbers up to four-digits by two-digits.	11, 12	
Solve application problems involving whole number operations.	13	
Use simple ratios to describe problem situations.	14	
Identify odd and even numbers.	15	
Identify factors of whole numbers.	16	
Apply basic properties of operations.	17	
Measurement		
Identify the attribute that is appropriate to measure in a given situation.	18	
Select or use appropriate measurement instruments such as ruler, meter stick, clock, thermometer, or other scaled instruments.	19	
Solve problems involving perimeter of plane figures, providing the formula as part of the problem.	20	
Solve problems involving area of rectangles, providing the formula as part of the problem.	21	
Select or use appropriate type of unit for the attribute being measured such as length, time, or temperature.	22	
Geometry		
Describe real world objects using simple plane figures (e.g., triangles, rectangles, squares and circles) and simple solid figures (e.g., cubes, spheres, and cylinders).	23	
Identify or draw angles and other geometric figures in the plane.	24	
Describe attributes of two- and three-dimensional shapes.	25	
Recognize two-dimensional faces of three-dimensional shapes.	26	
Data Analysis and Probability		
Interpret pictograms, bar graphs, circle graphs, line graphs, line plots, tables, and tallies.	27	

Mathematics Concepts	Test Item(s)	Proficient? Yes or No
Data Analysis and Probability *(continued)*		
Read or interpret a single set of data.	28	
List all possible outcomes of a given situation or event.	29	
Represent the probability of a given outcome.	30	
Algebra		
Recognize, describe, or extend numerical patterns.	31	
Find the value of the unknown in a whole number sentence.	32, 33, 36	
Express simple mathematical relationships using number sentences.	34	
Graph or interpret points with whole number or letter coordinates on grids or in the first quadrant of the coordinate plane.	35	

Student Comments: _____

_____

_____

_____

_____

_____

_____

Parent Comments: _____

_____

_____

_____

_____

_____

_____

Teacher Comments: _____

_____

_____

_____

_____

_____

_____

Benchmark Test 1 Report

Mathematics Concepts	NAEP Objective(s)	Test Items	Number Correct	Proficient? Yes or No	Skills Review and Practice
Integers and Algebraic Expressions					
Apply basic properties of operations when working with algebraic expressions.	N5e	1, 2, 3	☐/3		209
Find or model absolute value and apply absolute value to problem situations; to order rational numbers.	N1a, g, i	4, 5, 6	☐/3		211
Perform computations involving integers.	N3a	7, 8, 9	☐/3		212, 213
Apply basic properties of operations.	N5e	10, 11, 12	☐/3		216
Solve one-step equations with rational coefficients symbolically or graphically.	A4a,c	13, 14, 15	☐/3		217, 221
Rational Numbers					
Recognize and translate between different forms of rational numbers (i.e., fractions, decimals, and percents).	N1e	16, 17, 18	☐/3		236
Order or compare rational numbers (fractions, decimals, percents, integers) using various representations.	N1i	19, 20, 21	☐/3		237
Perform addition and subtraction computations with rational numbers.	N3a	22, 23, 24	☐/3		238
Perform multiplication and division computations with rational numbers.	N3a	25, 26, 27	☐/3		239
Perform basic operations using powers and exponents.	A3b	28, 29, 30	☐/3		265
Express or interpret numbers using scientific notation from real-world contexts.	N1f	31, 32, 33	☐/3		262

*NAEP (National Assessment of Educational Progress Mathematics Objectives)

N = Number Properties and Operations; M = Measurement; G = Geometry; D = Data Analysis and Probability; A = Algebra

Student Comments: _____
_____
_____
_____
_____
_____
_____
_____
_____

Parent Comments: _____
_____
_____
_____
_____
_____
_____
_____
_____

Teacher Comments: _____
_____
_____
_____
_____
_____
_____
_____
_____

Name _____ Class _____ Date _____

Benchmark Test 2 Report

Mathematics Concepts	NAEP Objective(s)	Test Items	Number Correct	Proficient? Yes or No	Skills Review and Practice
Real Numbers and the Coordinate Plane					
Use ordered pairs to graph and interpret points on a coordinate plane.	A2c	1, 2, 3	☐/3		302, 303
Translate between or interpret tables, graphs, and equations representing linear relationships.	A2b	4, 5, 6	☐/3		305
Solve system of equations problems involving coordinate pairs on the rectangular coordinate system.	A2c, d	7, 8, 9	☐/3		231
Identify lines of symmetry in plane figures and classify types of symmetry of plane figures.	G2a	10, 11, 12	☐/3		233
Perform transformations on figures and recognize the effect of a transformation on a figure.	G2c	13, 14, 15	☐/3		232
Estimate square roots of numbers between two whole numbers.	N2d	16, 17, 18	☐/3		242
Applications of Proportions					
Use fractions to represent and express ratios and proportions.	N4b	19, 20, 21	☐/3		244
Convert measurements within the customary and metric systems.	M2b	22, 23, 24	☐/3		245
Use appropriate strategies in solving proportions.	N4c	25, 26, 27	☐/3		247
Use proportional reasoning to solve problems involving similarity and indirect measurement.	G2e, f	28, 29, 30	☐/3		248, 249
Construct or solve problems involving scale models and maps.	M2f	31, 32, 33	☐/3		250

*NAEP (National Assessment of Educational Progress Mathematics Objectives)

 N = Number Properties and Operations; M = Measurement; G = Geometry; D = Data Analysis and Probability; A = Algebra

Student Comments: _____

_____

_____

_____

_____

_____

_____

_____

_____

_____

Parent Comments: _____

_____

_____

_____

_____

_____

_____

_____

_____

_____

_____

Teacher Comments: _____

_____

_____

_____

_____

_____

_____

_____

_____

_____

Benchmark Test 3 Report

Mathematics Concepts	NAEP Objective(s)	Test Items	Number Correct	Proficient? Yes or No	Skills Review and Practice
Applications of Percent					
Recognize and translate between multiple representations of rational numbers (fractions, decimals, percents).	N1e	1, 2, 3	□/3		253
Solve problems involving percentages.	N4d	4, 5, 6	□/3		255, 256
Solve problems involving percent of change relationships.	N4d	7, 8, 9	□/3		257
Solve percent problems involving markup and discount.	N4d	10, 11, 12	□/3		258
Solve percent problems involving simple and compound interest.	N4d	13, 14, 15	□/3		260
Analyze situations that involve probability and determine probability of simple events in familiar contexts.	D4a, b	16, 17, 18	□/3		197
Equations and Inequalities					
Solve two-step equations with rational coefficients symbolically or graphically.	A4a, c	19, 20, 21	□/3		218
Write algebraic expressions to represent a real-world situation and simplify the expression using basic operations.	A3a, b	22, 23, 24	□/3		221
Solve multi-step equations with rational coefficients symbolically or graphically.	A4a, c	25, 26, 27, 28, 29, 30	□/6		220
Solve one-step inequalities with rational coefficients symbolically or graphically.	A4a, c	31, 32, 33	□/3		222, 223
Solve multi-step inequalities with rational coefficients symbolically or graphically.	A4a, c	34, 35, 36	□/3		224

*NAEP (National Assessment of Educational Progress Mathematics Objectives)

N = Number Properties and Operations; M = Measurement; G = Geometry; D = Data Analysis and Probability; A = Algebra

Student Comments: _____

_____

_____

_____

_____

_____

_____

_____

_____

_____

Parent Comments: _____

_____

_____

_____

_____

_____

_____

_____

_____

_____

Teacher Comments: _____

_____

_____

_____

_____

_____

_____

_____

_____

_____

Name_____ Class_____ Date_____

Benchmark Test 4 Report

Mathematics Concepts	NAEP Objective(s)	Test Items	Number Correct	Proficient? Yes or No	Skills Review and Practice
Geometry					
Describe or analyze properties involving special pairs of angles.	G3b, g	1, 2, 3	☐/3		268
Apply geometric properties involving angles and parallel lines.	G3b, g	4, 5, 6	☐/3		269
Justify congruence relationships between plane figures.	G2e	7, 8, 9	☐/3		270
Analyze side and angle properties to classify triangles and quadrilaterals.	G3f	10, 11, 12	☐/3		272
Analyze angles between various polygonal plane figures.	G3f	13, 14, 15	☐/3		273
Solve mathematical or real-world problems involving circumference or area of circles or area of polygons.	M1h	16, 17, 18	☐/3		274, 275
Measurement					
Describe and identify solids.	G1c	19, 20, 21	☐/3		277
Represent or describe a three-dimensional situation using nets and three-dimensional figures.	G1e	22, 23, 24	☐/3		279
Solve mathematical or real-world problems involving the surface areas of various solids.	M1j	25, 26, 27	☐/3		280, 281
Solve mathematical or real-world problems involving the volumes of prisms and cylinders.	M1j	28, 29, 30	☐/3		282
Solve mathematical or real-world problems involving the volumes of pyramids and cones.	M1j	31, 32, 33	☐/3		283
Apply geometric properties and relationships in solving problems involving similar solids.	G3b	34, 35, 36	☐/3		285

*NAEP (National Assessment of Educational Progress Mathematics Objectives)

N = Number Properties and Operations; M = Measurement; G = Geometry; D = Data Analysis and Probability; A = Algebra

Student Comments: _____
_____
_____
_____
_____
_____
_____
_____
_____
_____
_____

Parent Comments: _____
_____
_____
_____
_____
_____
_____
_____
_____
_____
_____

Teacher Comments: _____
_____
_____
_____
_____
_____
_____
_____
_____
_____
_____

Benchmark Test 5 Report

Mathematics Concepts	NAEP Objective(s)	Test Items	Number Correct	Proficient? Yes or No	Skills Review and Practice
Using Graphs to Analyze Data					
Calculate, use, or interpret the mean, median, or mode.	D2a	1, 2, 3	☐/3		214
Given a graph or a set of data, compare the effectiveness of different representations of the same data.	D1a, c, e	4, 5, 6	☐/3		292
Use and interpret Venn diagrams.		7, 8, 9	☐/3		293
Read, construct, and investigate graphs and then solve a problem using the data in the graphs.	D1a, d, D2a	10, 11, 12, 13, 14, 15, 16, 17, 18	☐/9		286, 287 288, 289 290, 291
Read and interpret data, including interpolating and extrapolating from data.	D1a, D2e	19, 20, 21	☐/3		286, 287 288, 289 290, 291
Compare and contrast the effectiveness of different graphical representations of the same data.	D1e	22, 23, 24	☐/3		286, 287 288, 289 290, 291
Probability					
Distinguish between experimental and theoretical probability and estimate the probability of simple and compound events through experimentation or simulation.	D4c, d	25, 26, 27, 28, 29, 30	☐/6		197
Given a sample, identify possible sources of bias in sampling; distinguish between a random and non-random sample and evaluate the design of an experiment.	D3a, b, c	31, 32, 33	☐/3		300
Distinguish between independent and dependent events and determine the probability of independent and dependent events.	D4a, h	34, 35, 36	☐/3		198

Mathematics Concepts	NAEP Objective(s)	Test Items	Number Correct	Proficient? Yes or No	Skills Review and Practice
Find or model permutations and apply permutations to problem situations.	D4f	37, 38, 39	$\frac{\square}{3}$		195
Find or model combinations and apply combinations to problem situations.	D4f	40, 41, 42	$\frac{\square}{3}$		196

*NAEP (National Assessment of Educational Progress Mathematics Objectives)

N = Number Properties and Operations; M = Measurement; G = Geometry; D = Data Analysis and Probability; A = Algebra

Student Comments: _____

_____

_____

_____

_____

_____

_____

Parent Comments: _____

_____

_____

_____

_____

_____

_____

Teacher Comments: _____

_____

_____

_____

_____

_____

_____

_____

NAEP Mathematics Assessment Framework

NUMBER PROPERTIES AND OPERATIONS	TEST ITEMS
1) Number sense	
a) Use place value to model and describe integers and decimals.	
b) Model or describe rational numbers or numerical relationships using number lines and diagrams.	69
d) Write or rename rational functions.	20
e) Recognize, translate between, or apply multiple representations of rational numbers in meaningful contexts.	
f) Express or interpret numbers using scientific notation from real life contexts.	17
g) Find or model absolute value or apply to problem situations.	
i) Order or compare rational numbers using various models and representations.	4
j) Order or compare rational numbers including very large and small integers, and decimals and fractions close to zero.	
2) Estimation	
a) Establish or apply benchmarks for rational numbers and common irrational numbers in contexts.	
b) Make estimates appropriate to a given situation by: identifying when estimation is appropriate, determinating the level of accuracy needed, selecting the appropriate method of estimation, or analyzing the effect of an estimation method on the accuracy of results.	1
c) Verify solutions or determine the reasonableness of results in a variety of situations including calculator and computer results.	
d) Estimate square or cube roots of numbers less than 1,000 between two whole numbers.	2
3) Number operations	
a) Perform computations with rational numbers.	23, 24, 26
d) Describe the effect of multiplying and dividing by numbers.	
e) Provide a mathematical argument to explain operations with two or more fractions.	
f) Interpret rational number operations and the relationship between them.	
g) Solve application problems involving rational numbers and operations using exact answers or estimates as appropriate.	21, 22
4) Ratios and proportional reasoning	
a) Use ratios to describe problem situations.	27
b) Use fractions to represent and express ratios and proportions.	29, 30
c) Use proportional reasoning to model and solve problems.	28, 32, 33
d) Solve problems involving percentages.	34, 35, 36, 37
5) Properties of number and operations	
a) Describe odd and even integers and how they behave under different operations.	
b) Recognize, find, or use factors, multiples, or prime factorization.	19, 67
c) Recognize or use prime and composite numbers to solve problems.	
d) Use divisibility or remainders in problem settings.	18
e) Apply basic properties of operations.	
f) Explain or justify a mathematical concept or relationship.	

MEASUREMENT	TEST ITEMS
1) Measuring physical attributes	
b) Compare objects with respect to length, area, volume, angle measurement, weight, or mass.	48
c) Estimate the size of an object with respect to a given measurement attribute.	
g) Select or use appropriate measurement instrument to determine or create a given length, area, volume, angle, weight, or mass.	25
h) Solve mathematical or real-world problems involving perimeter or area of plane figures such as triangles, rectangles, circles, or composite figures.	49, 50, 51
j) Solve problems involving volume or surface area of rectangular solids, cylinders, prisms, or composite shapes.	53, 66
k) Solve problems involving indirect measurement such as finding the height of a building by comparing its shadow with the height and shadow of a known object.	31
l) Solve problems involving rates such as speed or population density.	
2) Systems of measurement	
a) Select or use appropriate type of unit for the attribute being measured such as length, area, angle, time, or volume.	
b) Solve problems involving conversions within the same measurement system such as conversions involving square inches and square feet.	
c) Estimate the measure of an object in one system given the measure of that object in another system and the approximate conversion factor.	3
d) Determine appropriate size of unit of measurement in problem situation involving such attributes as length, area, or volume.	
e) Determine appropriate accuracy of measurement in problem situations and find the measure to that degree of accuracy.	
f) Construct or solve problems involving scale drawings.	

GEOMETRY	TEST ITEMS
1) Dimension and shape	
a) Draw or describe a path of shortest length between points to solve problems in context.	
b) Identify a geometric object given written description of its properties.	42, 46
c) Identify, define, or describe geometric shapes in the plane and in 3-dimensional space given a visual representation.	39, 41
d) Draw or sketch from a written description polygons, circles, or semicircles.	
e) Represent or describe a three-dimensional situation in a two-dimensional drawing using perspective.	
f) Demonstrate an understanding about the two- and three-dimensional shapes in our world through identifying, drawing, modeling, building, or taking apart.	43
2) Transformation of shapes and preservation of properties	
a) Identify lines of symmetry in plane figures or recognize and classify types of symmetries of plane figures.	
c) Recognize or informally describe the effect of a transformation on two-dimensional geometric shapes.	

GEOMETRY continued	TEST ITEMS
d) Predict results of combining, subdividing, and changing shapes of place figures and solids	
e) Justify relationships of congruence and similarity, and apply these relationships using scaling and proportional reasoning.	
f) For similar figures, identify and use the relationships of conservation of angle and of proportionality of side length and perimeter.	45
3) Relationships between geometric figures	
b) Apply geometric properties and relationships in solving simple problems in two- and three-dimensions.	28, 40, 48
c) Represent problem situations with simple geometric models to solve mathematical or real-world problems.	
d) Use the Pythagorean theorem to solve problems.	52, 70
f) Describe or analyze simple properties of, or relationships between, triangles, quadrilaterals, and other polygonal plane figures.	44
g) Describe or analyze properties and relationships of parallel or intersecting lines.	
4) Position and direction	
a) Describe relative positions of points and lines using the geometric ideas of midpoint, points on common line through a common point, parallelism, or perpendicularity.	
b) Describe the intersection of two or more geometric figures in the plane.	
c) Visualize or describe the cross-section of a solid.	
d) Represent geometric figures using rectangular coordinates on a plane.	
5) Mathematical reasoning	
a) Make and test a geometric conjecture about regular polygons.	
DATA ANALYSIS AND PROBABILITY	**TEST ITEMS**
1) Data representation	
a) Read or interpret data, including interpolating or extrapolating from data.	47, 68
b) Given a set of data, complete a graph and then solve a problem using the data in the graph (circle graphs, histograms, bar graphs, line graphs, scatterplots).	
c) Solve problems by estimating and computing with data from a single set or across sets of data.	
d) Given a graph or a set of data, determine whether information is represented effectively and appropriately (circle graphs, histograms, bar graphs, line graphs, scatterplots).	
e) Compare and contrast the effectiveness of different representations of the same data.	
2) Characteristics of data sets	
a) Calculate, use, or interpret mean, median, mode, or range.	5
b) Describe how mean, median, mode, range, or interquartile ranges relate to the shape of distribution.	6
c) Identify outliers and determine their effect on mean, median, mode, or range.	
d) Using appropriate statistical measures, compare two or more data sets describing the same characteristic for two different populations or subsets of the same population.	

DATA ANALYSIS AND PROBABILITY continued	TEST ITEMS
e) Visually choose the line that best fits given a scatterplot and informally explain the meaning of the line. Use the line to make predictions.	
3) Experiments and samples	
a) Given a sample, identify possible sources of bias in sampling.	
b) Distinguish between a random and non-random sample.	61
d) Evaluate the design of an experiment.	
4) Probability	
a) Analyze a situation that involves probability of an independent event.	
b) Determine the theoretical probability of simple and compound events in familiar contexts.	62
c) Estimate the probability of simple and compound events through experimentation or simulation.	
d) Distinguish between experimental and theoretical probability.	63
e) Determine the sample space for a given situation.	
f) Use a sample space to determine the probability of the possible outcomes of an event.	
g) Represent probability using fractions, decimals, and percents.	
h) Determine the probability of independent and dependent events.	
j) Interpret probabilities within a given context.	
ALGEBRA	TEST ITEMS
1) Patterns, relations, and functions	
a) Recognize, describe, or extend numerical and geometric patterns using tables, graphs, words, or symbols.	54, 60
b) Generalize a pattern appearing in a numerical sequence or table or graph using words or symbols.	55
c) Analyze or create patterns, sequences, or linear functions given a rule.	64
e) Identify functions as linear or non-linear or contrast distinguishing properties of function from tables, graphs, or equations.	59
f) Interpret the meaning of slope or intercepts in linear functions.	58, 68
2) Algebraic representations	
a) Translate between different representations of linear expressions using symbols, graphs, tables, diagrams, or written descriptions.	56
b) Analyze or interpret linear relationships expressed in symbols, graphs, tables, diagrams, or written descriptions.	
c) Graph or interpret points that are represented by ordered pairs of numbers on a rectangular coordinate system.	
d) Solve problems involving coordinate pairs on the rectangular coordinate system.	57
e) Make, validate, and justify conclusions and generalizations about linear relationships.	
g) Identify or represent functional relationships in meaningful contexts including proportional, linear, and common non-linear in tables, graphs, words, or symbols.	

ALGEBRA continued	TEST ITEMS
3) Variables, expressions, and operations	
a) Write algebraic expressions, equations, or inequalities to represent the situation.	7, 9, 14
b) Perform basic operations, using appropriate tools, on linear algebraic expressions.	8
4) Equations and inequalities	
a) Solve linear equations or inequalities.	12, 15, 16
b) Interpret "=" as an equivalence between two expressions and use this interpretation to solve problems.	
c) Analyze situations or solve problems using linear equations and inequalities with rational coefficients symbolically or graphically.	10, 11, 13
d) Interpret relationships between symbolic linear expressions and graphs of lines by identifying and computing slope and intercepts.	
e) Use and evaluate common formulas.	

Correlation Chart: Practice Test to the SAT 10 Standards for Grade 8

SAT 10 Standards for Grade 8	Process Clusters	Test Items
MATHEMATICS: PROBLEM SOLVING		
Number Sense and Operations		
Identify number expressed in scientific notation.	Communication and Representation	9
Identify alternative representations of rational numbers.		3, 4, 5, 8
Identify and use order of operation rules.		
Round decimal numbers to a specified place value.		
Compare and order rational numbers.	Estimation	1, 2
Identify alternative representations of rational numbers.		3, 4, 5, 8
Identify least common multiple or greatest common factor for a set of numbers.		
Solve problems using estimation strategies.		42
Compare and order rational numbers.	Mathematical Connections	1, 2
Identify and use field properties of addition and multiplication.		
Identify alternative representations of real numbers.		3, 4, 5, 8
Translate between visual representations, sentences, and symbolic notation.		
Compare and order real numbers.	Reasoning and Problem Solving	2
Solve problems using numerical reasoning.		47, 48
Solve problems using appropriate strategies.		17, 21, 49, 50, 51
Solve problems using estimations strategies.		
Solve problems using nonroutine strategies.		
Patterns, Relationships, and Algebra		
Evaluate expressions.	Mathematical Connections	11
Identify graphs of inequalities.		14
Translate problem situations into algebraic equations and expressions.		12
Solve algebraic equations, problems involving patterns, and problems involving ratio or proportion.	Reasoning and Problem Solving	15, 16, 20, 21, 46
Data Analysis and Probability		
Read and interpret tables and graphs.	Communication and Representation	18
Read and interpret tables and graphs.	Estimation	24, 25, 26, 27
Analyze tables and graphs.		
Identify possible outcomes.		
Determine and use measures of central tendency.	Mathematical Connections	23, 24
Read and interpret tables and graphs.		24, 25, 26, 27
Determine combinations and permutations.		19
Identify probabilities of simple events.	Reasoning and Problem Solving	22

SAT 10 Standards for Grade 8	Process Clusters	Test Items
Geometry and Measurement		
Identify parallel and perpendicular lines.	Mathematical Connections	29
Identify a radius, diameter, or chord of a given circle.		28
Solve problems using properties of geometric figures.		29, 30, 36, 37, 52
Solve problems using spatial reasoning.		35, 38
Determine measurements indirectly from scale drawings.		47
Solve problems involving perimeter, circumference, area, or volume.	Estimation	43
Convert between units of measurement.	Reasoning and Problem Solving	39, 41, 45
Solve problems involving perimeter, circumference, area, or volume.		31, 32, 33, 34, 40
MATHEMATICS: PROCEDURES		
Computation with Whole Numbers		
Addition of whole numbers using symbolic notation.		
Addition of whole numbers in context.		11, 24, 25
Subtraction of whole numbers using symbolic notation.		
Subtraction of whole numbers in context.		23
Multiplication of whole numbers using symbolic notation.		
Multiplication of whole numbers in context.		6, 24, 25
Division of whole numbers using symbolic notation.		
Division of whole numbers in context.		9, 10, 17, 23
Computation with Decimals		
Addition of decimals using symbolic notation.		1
Addition of decimals in context.		29
Subtraction of decimals using symbolic notation.		
Subtraction of decimals in context.		
Multiplication of decimals using symbolic notation.		3
Multiplication of decimals in context.		16, 28
Division of decimals using symbolic notation.		7
Division of decimals in context.		12, 29
Computation with Fractions		
Addition of fractions using symbolic notation.		5
Addition of fractions in context.		
Subtraction of fractions using symbolic notation.		2
Subtraction of fractions in context.		13, 14, 19
Multiplication of fractions using symbolic notation.		22, 26
Multiplication of fractions in context.		15, 18, 20, 23
Division of fractions using symbolic notation.		4
Division of fractions in context.		21

Correlation Chart: Practice Test to the ITBS Standards

ITBS CONCEPT	TEST ITEM(S)
NUMBER PROPERTIES AND OPERATIONS	
Represent numbers	24
Order numbers	1, 16
Apply properties of numbers	
Classify numbers by divisibility	8, 12
Perform operations	6
Write numbers in exponential form	14
ALGEBRA	
Use and interpret operational symbols	
Use and interpret relational symbols	4
Solve equations	15, 22, 36, 38
Use expressions to model a situation	37
Explore numerical patterns	13
GEOMETRY	
Compare geometric figures	25
Identify geometric figures	
Describe geometric properties	
Describe geometric relationships	
Apply the concept of area	10
Apply the concept of volume	40
MEASUREMENT	
Measure time	
Measure weight	
Identify appropriate units	
PROBABILITY AND STATISTICS	
Apply probability concepts	21
Apply counting rules	29
Apply measures of central tendency	32
Apply measures of variability	
ESTIMATION	
Use standard rounding	
Use order of magnitude	
Use number sense	30, 33
PROBLEM SOLVING	
Multiple-step	20
Approaches and procedures	5

ITBS CONCEPT	TEST ITEM(S)
DATA INTERPRETATION	
Read amounts	34
Compare quantities	
Interpret relations and trends	7, 28
COMPUTE WITH WHOLE NUMBERS	
Add with regrouping	2
Subtract with regrouping	
Multiply with regrouping	23
Multiply without regrouping	19
Divide with a remainder	
ADD AND SUBTRACT WITH FRACTIONS	
Add fractions with different denominators	9
Subtract fractions with different denominators	18, 26
MULTIPLY WITH FRACTIONS	
Multiply a fraction with a whole number	27
Multiply two simple fractions	39
DIVIDE WITH FRACTIONS	
Divide a fraction by a whole number	
Divide two simple fractions	
ADD AND SUBTRACT WITH DECIMALS	
Add decimals with the same number of decimal places	
Add decimals with different number of decimal places	31
Subtract decimals with the same number of decimal places	3
MULTIPLY WITH DECIMALS	
Multiply a decimal number and a whole number	11, 17
Multiply two decimals	35

Correlation Chart: Practice Test to TerraNova for Grade 8

TERRANOVA OBJECTIVES FOR GRADE 8	TEST ITEM(S)
PARTS 1 AND 2	
10 Number and Number Relations • Demonstrate an understanding of number, number sense, and number theory by ordering numbers, representing numbers in equivalent forms, identifying relationships, interpreting numbers in real-world situations, and applying number concepts in real-world situations.	4, 5, 11, 13, 14, 16, 17, 18, 55
11 Computation and Numerical Estimation • Demonstrate proficiency in computation procedures, solve real-world computation problems, apply a variety of estimation strategies, and determine reasonableness of results.	54
12 Operation Concepts • Demonstrate an understanding of the properties and relationships of operations, relate mathematical representations to problem situations, and apply operational processes to solve problems	12, 15
13 Measurement • Demonstrate an understanding of measurement systems, units, and tools by describing, calculating, or estimating size, location, and time; by using the concepts of perimeter, area, volume, capacity, weight, and mass; and by identifying appropriate degrees of accuracy. • Solve problems involving principles of measurement, rate, and scale.	6, 19, 21, 22, 25, 46, 49, 50, 52, 53, 56
14 Geometry and Spatial Sense • Demonstrate spatial sense and an understanding of geometry by visualizing and identifying two- and three- dimensional objects, classifying shapes, recognizing symmetry, using transformations, applying geometric formulas, and evaluating properties of geometric figures.	10, 23, 34, 44, 45, 47, 48, 51
15 Data Analysis, Statistics and Probability • Analyze, interpret, and evaluate data in various forms; and apply the concepts and processes of data analysis, statistics, and probability to real-world situations.	30, 36, 37, 38, 39, 40, 41, 42, 43
16 Patterns, Functions, Algebra • Recognize and extend patterns. • Demonstrate an understanding of functional relationships, algebraic processes, variables, and inequality. • Recognize algebraic representations of problem situations and apply algebraic methods to solve real-world problems.	7, 8, 20, 24, 26, 27, 28, 29, 31, 32, 33, 35
17 Problem Solving and Reasoning • Select and apply problem-solving strategies, identify necessary information, use patterns and relationships to evaluate situations, apply inductive and deductive reasoning and spatial and proportional reasoning, and solve a variety of non-routine, real-world problems.	9

TERRANOVA OBJECTIVES FOR GRADE 8	TEST ITEM(S)
PART 3	
43 Add Whole Numbers • Add whole numbers.	
44 Subtract Whole Numbers • Subtract whole numbers.	
45 Multiply Whole Numbers • Multiply whole numbers.	
46 Divide Whole Numbers • Divide whole numbers.	
47 Decimals • Add, subtract, multiply, and divide decimals.	2, 17
48 Fractions • Add, subtract, multiply, and divide fractions.	6, 7, 8, 9
49 Integers • Add, subtract, multiply, and divide integers.	4, 5, 10, 12
50 Percents • Solve computational problems involving percents.	1, 13, 15, 18
51 Order of Operations • Solve computational problems involving the standard order of operations.	3, 14, 19, 20
52 Algebraic Operations • Solve computational problems involving exponents, roots, absolute value, and algebraic expressions and equations.	11, 16

Answers

Screening Test 1

1. B **2.** C **3.** D **4.** D **5.** C **6.** B **7.** B **8.** B **9.** A **10.** A
11. C **12.** D **13.** B **14.** B **15.** C **16.** B **17.** C **18.** D
19. B **20.** C **21.** D **22.** C **23.** B **24.** D **25.** C **26.** D
27. B **28.** C **29.** D **30.** C **31.** D **32.** C **33.** D **34.** A
35. D **36.** A

Benchmark Test 1

1. B **2.** H **3.** B **4.** J **5.** C **6.** G **7.** B **8.** J **9.** B **10.** J
11. C **12.** G **13.** C **14.** F **15.** D **16.** F **17.** D **18.** G
19. A **20.** H **21.** B **22.** J **23.** A **24.** F **25.** D **26.** H
27. B **28.** H **29.** B **30.** H **31.** C **32.** H **33.** B **34.** H
35. A **36.** J

Benchmark Test 2

1. D **2.** G **3.** B **4.** H **5.** B **6.** H **7.** A **8.** F **9.** A
10. H **11.** A **12.** G **13.** D **14.** J **15.** A **16.** H **17.** B
18. H **19.** C **20.** H **21.** A **22.** H **23.** D **24.** J **25.** A
26. F **27.** A **28.** G **29.** D **30.** G **31.** D **32.** J **33.** A

Benchmark Test 3

1. B **2.** G **3.** D **4.** H **5.** B **6.** H **7.** B **8.** J **9.** C
10. F **11.** D **12.** H **13.** C **14.** H **15.** D **16.** J **17.** C
18. G **19.** A **20.** G **21.** A **22.** F **23.** C **24.** G **25.** C
26. F **27.** A **28.** H **29.** B **30.** J **31.** C **32.** G **33.** A
34. H **35.** A **36.** J

Benchmark Test 4

1. B **2.** G **3.** A **4.** H **5.** C **6.** J **7.** C **8.** G **9.** D
10. J **11.** C **12.** H **13.** C **14.** J **15.** D **16.** G **17.** B
18. H **19.** A **20.** H **21.** A **22.** H **23.** C **24.** G **25.** D
26. J **27.** D **28.** G **29.** B **30.** H **31.** A **32.** F **33.** D
34. H **35.** C **36.** J

Benchmark Test 5

1. A **2.** F **3.** C **4.** F **5.** D **6.** J **7.** B **8.** F **9.** B
10. G **11.** D **12.** G **13.** C **14.** G **15.** D **16.** H **17.** B
18. H **19.** A **20.** G **21.** D **22.** G **23.** A **24.** H
25. D **26.** J **27.** D **28.** F **29.** B **30.** J **31.** A **32.** F
33. C **34.** H **35.** D **36.** F **37.** C **38.** H **39.** D **40.** G
41. D **42.** H

Quarter 1 Test, Form A

1. 48 **2.** 33 units **3.** < **4.** -138 feet **5.** $-\frac{1}{2}$ **6.** 9 **7.** -19
8. $-4m + 24$ **9.** -242 **10.** $3^4 \cdot x^3 \cdot y^2$ **11.** $x = -11$
12. $n = 44$ **13.** $p = -15$ **14.** $13x - 40$ **15.** $26, 32, 40, 16$
16. 5 **17.** The GCF of 81 and 108 is 27. Divide numerator and
denominator by 27 to get $\frac{3}{4}$. **18.** .700 **19.** $1\frac{7}{20}$ **20.** -3.4 **21.** $\frac{4}{9}$

22. $2 \cdot 3^2 \cdot 7$

23. $-2\frac{4}{5}, -1.25, -0.63, 0.34, \frac{3}{8}$ **24.** < **25.** 6 cups **26.** $6\frac{5}{48}$
27. 6 **28.** $2\frac{1}{2}$ **29.** $P = 38$ **30.** $x = \sqrt{89} \approx 9.4$ **31.** no
32. $\sqrt{18} = \sqrt{9}\sqrt{2} = 3\sqrt{2}$ **33.** 6
34. not linear

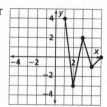

35. Answers will vary; any point (x, y) where $x > 0$ and $y < 0$
is correct. **36.** $(-6, -39)$ is not a solution of the equation.

37.

x	y
2	-3
4	-7
6	-11

38.
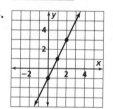

39.

40.
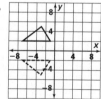

41. Quadrant III **42.** no lines of symmetry **43.** translation
44. 90°

Quarter 1 Test, Form B

1. 144 **2.** 42 units **3.** > **4.** $-33°$ **5.** $-\frac{1}{3}$ **6.** -46 **7.** -27
8. $-5m + 15$ **9.** -144 **10.** $4^3 \cdot x^2 \cdot y^2$ **11.** $y = -2$ **12.** $x = 72$

Answers (continued)

13. $w = -9$ **14.** $10x - 56$ **15.** $46, 44, 33, 16, 50$ **16.** 8 **17.** The GCF of 56 and 120 is 8. Divide numerator and denominator by 8 to get $\frac{7}{15}$. **18.** .800 **19.** $1\frac{19}{20}$ **20.** -2.5 **21.** $\frac{7}{9}$

22. $2^3 \cdot 3^2 \cdot 5$

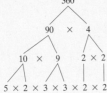

23. $-1.2, -0.97, \frac{4}{5}, 0.90, 4\frac{3}{5}$ **24.** $<$ **25.** $5\frac{1}{4}$ pt **26.** $1\frac{14}{15}$
27. $18\frac{1}{3}$ **28.** $1\frac{13}{15}$ **29.** $V = 300$ **30.** $x = \sqrt{244} \approx 15.6$
31. yes **32.** $\sqrt{196} = 14$ **33.** 7
34. linear

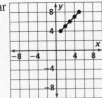

35. Answers will vary; any point (x, y) where $x < 0$ and $y < 0$ is correct. **36.** $(-4, -5)$ is not a solution of the equation.

37.

x	y
2	-4
4	-10
6	-16

38.

39.

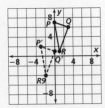

40.

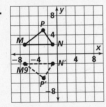

41. Quadrant III **42.** no lines of symmetry **43.** reflection
44. 180°

Quarter 1 Test, Form D

1. 48 **2.** 33 units **3.** $<$ **4.** -138 feet **5.** $-\frac{1}{2}$ **6.** 9 **7.** -19
8. $-4m + 24$ **9.** -242 **10.** $x = -11$ **11.** $n = 44$ **12.** $p = -15$
13. $13x - 40$ **14.** $26, 32, 40, 16$ **15.** 5 **16.** The GCF of 81 and 108 is 27. Divide numerator and denominator by 27 to get $\frac{3}{4}$.
17. .700 **18.** $1\frac{7}{20}$ **19.** $\frac{4}{9}$

20. $2 \cdot 3^2 \cdot 7$

21. $-2\frac{4}{5}, -1.25, -0.63, 0.34, \frac{3}{8}$ **22.** $<$ **23.** 6 cups **24.** $6\frac{5}{48}$
25. 6 **26.** $2\frac{1}{2}$ **27.** $P = 38$ **28.** $x = \sqrt{89} \approx 9.4$
29. $\sqrt{18} = \sqrt{9} \sqrt{2} = 3\sqrt{2}$

30. not linear

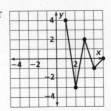

31. Answers will vary; any point (x, y) where $x > 0$ and $y < 0$ is correct. **32.** $(-6, -39)$ is not a solution of the equation.

33.

x	y
2	-3
4	-7
6	-11

34.

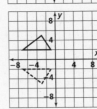

35.

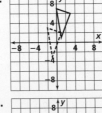

36. translation **37.** 90°

Quarter 1 Test, Form E

1. 144 **2.** 42 units **3.** $>$ **4.** $-33°$ **5.** $-\frac{1}{3}$ **6.** -46 **7.** -27
8. $-5m + 15$ **9.** -144 **10.** $y = -2$ **11.** $x = 72$ **12.** $w = -9$
13. $10x - 56$ **14.** $46, 44, 33, 16, 50$ **15.** 8 **16.** The GCF of 56 and 120 is 8. Divide numerator and denominator by 8 to get $\frac{7}{15}$.
17. .800 **18.** $1\frac{19}{20}$ **19.** $\frac{7}{9}$

Answers (continued)

20. $2^3 \cdot 3^2 \cdot 5$

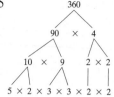

21. $-1.2, -0.97, \frac{4}{5}, 0.90, 4\frac{3}{5}$ **22.** $<$ **23.** $5\frac{1}{4}$ pt **24.** $1\frac{14}{15}$
25. $18\frac{1}{3}$ **26.** $1\frac{13}{15}$ **27.** $V = 300$ **28.** $x = \sqrt{244} \approx 15.6$
29. $\sqrt{196} = 14$

30. linear

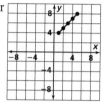

31. Answers will vary; any point (x, y) where $x < 0$ and $y < 0$ is correct. **32.** $(-4, -5)$ is not a solution of the equation.

33.

x	y
2	-4
4	-10
6	-16

34.

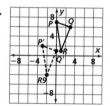

35.

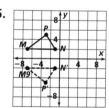

36. reflection **37.** $180°$

Quarter 2 Test, Form A

1. $5.30 per hour **2.** 30 mi/h **3.** 96; 132 **4.** $q = 39$
5. No; $\frac{18.6}{9.3} \neq \frac{9.4}{4.2}$ **6.** 18 **7.** $\frac{1}{4}$ **8.** 432 mi **9.** 15 ft
10. 0.375; 37.5% **11.** $\frac{23}{50}$ **12.** about 60 **13.** 54 **14.** 840
15. about 21% **16.** 45% **17.** $11.04 **18.** $142.20
19. $12.52 **20.** $45 **21.** $4025.60 **22.** $\frac{1}{3}$ **23.** $9\frac{1}{2}$ **24.** 182
25. 5 **26.** $3b + 16$ **27.** $x - 28$ **28.** $m = 3$ **29.** $z = -2\frac{1}{3}$
30. $p > 12$ **31.** $x \geq 7.255$ **32.** $x < -3$ **33.** $r > 14$
34. $w \geq -\frac{1}{2}$ **35.** $-48 > s$

Quarter 2 Test, Form B

1. 41 words/min **2.** 4 pt/min **3.** 240; 432 **4.** $x = 144$
5. No; $\frac{24}{25} \neq \frac{15}{16}$ **6.** 50 **7.** $\frac{9}{2}$ **8.** 270 mi **9.** 18 ft **10.** 0.14;
14% **11.** $\frac{9}{20}$ **12.** 90 **13.** 104 **14.** 1,300 **15.** 26%
16. 60% **17.** $15.99 **18.** $87.50 **19.** $35.71 **20.** $200
21. $6523 **22.** $\frac{1}{4}$ **23.** $e = 13.9$ **24.** $x = -7$ **25.** 6
26. $-5m + 32$ **27.** $5x - 33$ **28.** $n = 3$ **29.** $t = 2$
30. $y > 31$ **31.** $x \leq 5.6$ **32.** $x \geq -1$ **33.** $m < -40$
34. $s < 52$ **35.** $x \geq \frac{1}{4}$

Quarter 2 Test, Form D

1. $5.30 per hour **2.** 30 mi/h **3.** 96; 132 **4.** $q = 39$
5. No; $\frac{18.6}{9.3} \neq \frac{9.4}{4.2}$ **6.** 18 **7.** $\frac{1}{4}$ **8.** 432 mi **9.** 15 ft
10. 0.375; 37.5% **11.** $\frac{23}{50}$ **12.** about 60 **13.** 54 **14.** about
21% **15.** $11.04 **16.** $142.20 **17.** $45 **18.** $\frac{1}{3}$ **19.** $9\frac{1}{2}$
20. 182 **21.** 5 **22.** $x - 28$ **23.** $m = 3$ **24.** $p > 12$
25. $x < -3$ **26.** $r > 14$ **27.** $w \geq -\frac{1}{2}$

Quarter 2 Test, Form E

1. 41 words/min **2.** 4 pt/min **3.** 240; 432 **4.** $x = 144$
5. No; $\frac{24}{25} \neq \frac{15}{16}$ **6.** 50 **7.** $\frac{9}{2}$ **8.** 270 mi **9.** 18 ft **10.** 0.14; 14%
11. $\frac{9}{20}$ **12.** 90 **13.** 104 **14.** 60% **15.** $15.99 **16.** $87.50
17. $200 **18.** $\frac{1}{4}$ **19.** $e = 13.9$ **20.** $x = -7$ **21.** 6 **22.** $5x - 33$
23. $n = 3$ **24.** $y > 31$ **25.** $x \geq -1$ **26.** $m < -40$ **27.** $s < 52$

Quarter 3 Test, Form A

1. $\angle BFC$ or $\angle EFD$ **2.** $m\angle 1 = m\angle 3 = 145°, m\angle 2 = 35°$
3. $43°$ **4.** $52°$ **5.** $\angle 2$ and $\angle 6$, $\angle 3$ and $\angle 7$ **6.** $117°$ **7.** yes;
Angle-Side-Angle **8.** Check students' answers. **9.** parallelogram
10. $120°$ **11.** 103.2 dm^2 **12.** 56.52 cm **13.** $1,256$ m^2
14.

15.

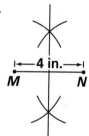

16. Sample answer: $\overleftrightarrow{FG}$ and $\overleftrightarrow{AE}$
17.

1	1	1
1	3	1
1	1	1

Answers (continued)

18.

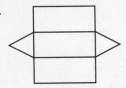

19. L.A. = 120 in.^{2}, S.A. = 138 in.^{2} **20.** S.A. = 75.36 cm^2, SA = 100.48 cm^2 **21.** V = 432 m^3 **22.** $V \approx 117.23$ in.^{3}

23. 283.5 m^3

24.

Shots Made	Frequency
1–2	2
3–4	2
5–6	4
7–8	1
9–10	1

25.

		X		
		X		
X	X	X		
X	X	X	X	X
1–2	3–4	5–6	7–8	9–10

26.

```
6 | 7
7 | 8
8 | 2 3 5 5 5 8 9
9 | 1 5
```
Key: 6 | 7 means 67.

Quarter 3 Test, Form B

1. ∠AFB or ∠CFD **2.** $m\angle 1 = m\angle 3 = 153°, m\angle 2 = 27°$
3. 34° **4.** 73° **5.** ∠1 and ∠5, ∠3 and ∠7, ∠2 and ∠6, ∠4 and ∠8
6. 67° **7.** yes; Side-Angle-Side **8.** Check students' answers.
9. rhombus **10.** 108° **11.** 6,230 in.^{2} **12.** 37.68 m **13.** 706.5 ft^2
14.

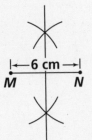

15.

16. Sample answer: $\overleftrightarrow{HE}$ and $\overleftrightarrow{GC}$

17.

3	4	3
1	1	1

18.

19. L.A. = 240 in.^{2}, S.A. = 290 in.^{2} **20.** L.A. = 276.32 cm^2, S.A. = 376.8 cm^2 **21.** V = 210 m^3 **22.** V = 640.56 cm^3

23. 33.6 yd^3

24.

Number of Shots	Frequency
1	1
2	3
3	1
4	3
5	2

25.

	X		X	
	X		X	X
X	X	X	X	X
1	2	3	4	5

26.

```
 7 | 8 9
 8 | 3 4 5
 9 | 0 1 5 9
10 | 1
```
Key: 7 | 8 means 78.

Quarter 3 Test, Form D

1. ∠BFC or ∠EFD **2.** $m\angle 1 = m\angle 3 = 145°, m\angle 2 = 35°$
3. 43° **4.** 52° **5.** ∠2 and ∠6, ∠3 and ∠7 **6.** 117° **7.** yes;
Angle-Side-Angle **8.** parallelogram **9.** 120° **10.** 103.2 dm^2
11. 56.52 cm **12.** 1,256 m^2
13.

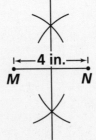

14.

15. Sample answer: $\overleftrightarrow{FG}$ and $\overleftrightarrow{AE}$

16.

1	1	1
1	3	1
1	1	1

Answers (continued)

17.

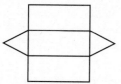

18. L.A. = 120 in.², S.A. = 138 in.² **19.** $V = 432$ m³

20.

Shots Made	Frequency
1–2	2
3–4	2
5–6	4
7–8	1
9–10	1

21.

```
        X
X   X   X
X   X   X   X   X
─────────────────────
1–2 3–4 5–6 7–8 9–10
```

22.

```
6 | 7
7 | 8
8 | 2 3 5 5 5 8 9
9 | 1 5
```
Key: 6 | 7 means 67.

Quarter 3 Test, Form E

1. $\angle AFB$ or $\angle CFD$ **2.** $m\angle 1 = m\angle 3 = 153°, m\angle 2 = 27°$
3. 34° **4.** 73° **5.** $\angle 1$ and $\angle 5, \angle 3$ and $\angle 7, \angle 2$ and $\angle 6, \angle 4$ and
$\angle 8$ **6.** 67° **7.** yes; Side-Angle-Side **8.** rhombus **9.** 108°
10. 6,230 in.² **11.** 37.68 m **12.** 706.5 ft²

13.

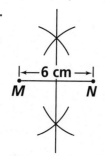

14.

15. Sample answer: $\overleftrightarrow{HE}$ and $\overleftrightarrow{GC}$

16.

3	4	3
1	1	1

17.

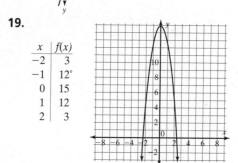

18. L.A. = 240 in², S.A. = 290 in²
19. $V = 210$ m³
20.

Number of Shots	Frequency
1	1
2	3
3	1
4	3
5	2

21.

```
    X           X
    X           X
X   X   X   X   X
────────────────────
1   2   3   4   5
```

22.

```
 7 | 8 9
 8 | 3 4 5
 9 | 0 1 5 9
10 | 1
```
Key: 7 | 8 means 78.

Quarter 4 Test, Form A

1. 54% **2.** $\frac{4}{5}$ or 80% **3.** Sample answer: Experimental
probability is based on data from experiments, while
theoretical probability examines all possible outcomes and is
based on theory. **4.** 9 **5.** no **6.** $\frac{1}{5}$ or 20% **7.** 720
8. 84 groups **9.** 56 **10.** $-6, -14, -22, -30$ **11.** 14
12. days 15–20 **13.** $f(-2) = 13$ **14.** $f(10) = -23$
15. $f(x) = .04x$ **16.** $-\frac{1}{9}$ **17.** -5
18.

19.

x	$f(x)$
-2	3
-1	12°
0	15
1	12
2	3

20. $-4b + 7a + 5$ **21.** $4b^2 + 3b + 5$ **22.** $a^2 + a + 2$
23. y^{13} **24.** 2.6^{13} **25.** x^3 **26.** w^{-12} **27.** $25x^6$
28. 40 seconds **29.** $6u^6 + 3u^5 - 6u^3$ **30.** 1

Answers (continued)

Quarter 4 Test, Form B

1. about 46% **2.** 77% **3.** Sample answer: Independent — when the outcome of the first event doesn't affect the outcome of the second event; Dependent — when the outcome of the first event does affect the outcome of the second event. **4.** 10 times a day **5.** yes **6.** $\frac{1}{3}$ or 33% **7.** 3,024 **8.** 495 **9.** 210 **10.** -1, $-7, -13, -19$ **11.** $-\frac{1}{2}$ **12.** days 20−25 **13.** 19 **14.** -14 **15.** $f(x) = 6x$ **16.** -3 **17.** 4

18.

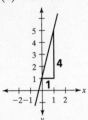

19.

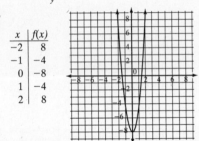

x	$f(x)$
-2	8
-1	-4
0	-8
1	-4
2	8

20. $-9k + 6m + 50$ **21.** $3a^3 - 3a^2 - 2a + 5$
22. $q^2 + 5q + 2$ **23.** x^{12} **24.** 1.4^{16} **25.** m^2 **26.** k^{-10}
27. $16b^{12}$ **28.** 50 seconds **29.** $14v^6 - 16v^5 + 8v^4$ **30.** $\frac{1}{4b}$

Quarter 4 Test, Form D

1. 80% **2.** Sample answer: Experimental probability is based on data from experiments, while theoretical probability examines all possible outcomes and is based on theory. **3.** 9 **4.** no
5. $\frac{1}{5}$ or 20% **6.** 720 **7.** 84 groups **8.** 56 **9.** $-6, -14, -22, -30$
10. 14 **11.** days 15−20 **12.** -23 **13.** $f(x) = .04x$ **14.** -3

15.

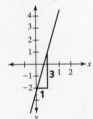

16.

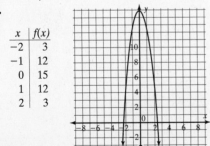

x	$f(x)$
-2	3
-1	12
0	15
1	12
2	3

17. $4b^2 + 3b + 5$ **18.** $a^2 + a + 2$ **19.** y^{13}
20. $6u^6 + 3u^5 - 6u^3$ **21.** x^3 **22.** 1 **23.** $25x^6$

Quarter 4 Test, Form E

1. 77% **2.** Sample answer: Independent — when the outcome of the first event doesn't affect the probability of the outcome of the second event; Dependent — when the outcome of the first event does affect the outcome of the second event. **3.** 10 times a day **4.** yes **5.** $\frac{1}{3}$ or 33% **6.** 3,024 **7.** 495 **8.** 210
9. $-1, -7, -13, -19$ **10.** $-\frac{1}{2}$ **11.** days 20−25 **12.** -14
13. $f(x) = 6x$ **14.** -3

15.

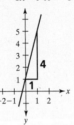

16.

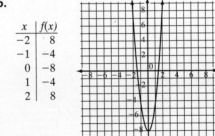

x	$f(x)$
-2	8
-1	-4
0	-8
1	-4
2	8

17. $3a^3 - 3a^2 - 2a + 5$ **18.** $q^2 + 5q + 2$ **19.** x^{12}
20. $14v^6 - 16v^5 + 8v^4$ **21.** m^2 **22.** $\frac{1}{4b}$ **23.** $16b^{12}$

Mid-Course Test, Form A

1. 63 **2.** 54 **3.** 3 **4.** $3 \cdot 2 + 3 \cdot 5$ **5.** $2n - 10$ **6.** 46 **7.** 6
8. $x \le 2$;

```
←——+———+———+———+———●——+——→
   -3 -2 -1   0   1   2   3
```

9. $x = 6$ **10.** $x = 60$ **11.** $x \le -1$ **12.** $5x \ge 40; x \ge 8$
13. $10x - 24$ **14.** $t = 4$ **15.** 3.48×10^6 **16.** 0.0000045
17. $A(-2, 2)$ $B(-4, -5)$ **18.** $(5, 12)$ **19.** Quadrant I
20.

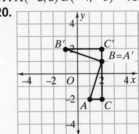

21. $x \le 48$

Answers (continued)

Test-Taking Strategies

Writing Gridded Responses

1. 55 **2.** 93 **3.** 38 **4.** 5.53 **5.** 32 **6.** 12

Writing Short Responses

1a. Sample answer: The first response received two points because it contains a correctly solved equation. The second response received one point because, although it is the correct answer, the student did not set up and solve an equation. The final response received 0 points because it does not have a correct equation and the equation is not solved correctly.
2. Sample answer: Let x = the price of one figurine.
$3x + 12.50 = 39.47; 3x = 26.97; x = 8.99$; Each figurine costs $8.99.

Writing Extended Responses

1.

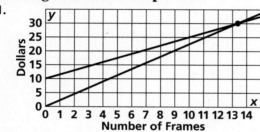

Sample Answer: Let x = the number of picture frames sold; Expenses equation: $y = 1.50x + 10.50$; Income equation: $y = 2.25x$. Solution: They must sell 14 picture frames to break even.
2. Sample answer: The student should receive 0 points because, even though the answer is correct, no procedure is shown.

Using a Variable

1. $\frac{9}{21} = \frac{30}{b}$; $b = 70$ blue marbles **2.** $\frac{2.5}{12} = \frac{w}{24}$; $w = 5$ cm;
$\frac{2.5}{12} = \frac{l}{30}$; $l = 6.25$ cm **3.** $\frac{3}{5} = \frac{g}{8.5}$; $g = 5.1$ ft **4.** $\frac{3}{195} = \frac{t}{520}$; $t = 8$ h
5. $\frac{18}{45} = \frac{28}{l}$; $l = 70$ m **6.** $\frac{1}{8} = \frac{3}{r}$; $r = 24$ ounces of red; $\frac{1}{8} = \frac{7}{b}$;
$b = 56$ ounces of blue; $\frac{1}{8} = \frac{6}{y}$; $y = 48$ ounces of yellow
7a. $\frac{2}{9} = \frac{7}{t}$; $t = 31.5$ h **7b.** $\frac{2}{9} = \frac{d}{15}$; $d = 3.\overline{3}$ or 3 *complete* dresses

Estimating the Answer

1. D **2.** G **3.** B **4.** J **5.** A **6.** G **7.** C **8.** G **9.** C
10. F

Reading for Understanding

1. 58.25 in. **2.** 11.12 in. **3.** Sample answer: The screen is not in the shape of a golden rectangle. The ratio of the longer side to the shorter side is $1.\overline{3}$, which is less than 1.618.

Drawing a Picture

1. 14 units **2.** parallelogram $RSUT$ $(6, 1)$ and parallelogram $RSTU$ $(-4, 1)$ **3.** rhombus **4.** no **5.** yes **6.** 607,904 yd^2
7. 10 blocks **8.** $l = 53$ cm, $w = 11$ cm

Eliminating Answers

1. Sample answer: Answer choices A and B can be eliminated because volume should be measured in cubic feet. The answer is either choice C or choice D. **2.** D **3.** F
4. C **5.** G **6.** A **7.** J

Measuring to Solve

1. 32 cm^2 **2.** 6.9 cm^2 **3.** 37.7 cm^2

Answering the Question Asked

1. B **2.** J **3.** A **4.** H **5.** A **6.** F **7.** A **8.** H

Interpreting Data

1. D **2.** F **3.** C **4.** H **5.** C **6.** H

Working Backward

1. B **2.** G **3.** A **4.** H **5.** B **6.** J **7.** C **8.** G **9.** A
10. G

Answers: NAEP Practice Test

1. C
2. D
3. E
4. E
5. A
6. B
7. D
8. D
9. C
10. C
11. D
12. B
13. E
14. D
15. E
16. B
17. C
18. E
19. B
20. A
21. D
22. C
23. A
24. B
25. C
26. D
27. E
28. D
29. D
30. C
31. B
32. E
33. C
34. C
35. D
36. D
37. E
38. D
39. E
40. C
41. B
42. A
43. A
44. E
45. D
46. C
47. C
48. B

49. B
50. C
51. B
52. C
53. E
54. C
55. B
56. E
57. A
58. B
59. A
60. A
61. C
62. E
63. B
64. Answers may vary. Sample: Find the pattern, $(n + 1)$, $(n + 2)$, $(n + 3)$, and so forth and continue the pattern until you arrive at the 10th term.
65. Check students' work.
66. 15.6 ft
67. 6 feet; 29 segments
68. Red and White
69. No; her answer can be tested by substitution: $x = -4$ and $y = -3$. $-4 < -3$ but $(-4)^2 > (-3)^2$ since $16 > 9$.
70. $1.69

Answers: SAT 10 Practice Test

Problem Solving

1. C
2. H
3. C
4. J
5. D
6. G
7. D
8. J
9. B
10. J
11. C
12. F
13. D
14. H
15. A
16. F
17. B
18. H
19. D
20. H
21. A
22. J
23. B
24. G
25. C
26. F
27. B
28. H
29. C
30. H
31. B
32. H
33. A
34. J
35. B
36. H
37. B
38. F
39. A
40. J
41. B
42. G
43. C
44. J
45. D
46. G
47. B
48. J
49. C
50. G
51. D
52. H

Procedures

1. C
2. F
3. A
4. K
5. C
6. F
7. B
8. H
9. C
10. H
11. E
12. F
13. B
14. F
15. B
16. H
17. A
18. G
19. B
20. F
21. A
22. G
23. C
24. F
25. E
26. G
27. A
28. G
29. E
30. J

Answers: ITBS Practice Test

1. B
2. F
3. B
4. H
5. D
6. G
7. A
8. G
9. C
10. F
11. B
12. F
13. C
14. J
15. B
16. J
17. C
18. F
19. B
20. H
21. A
22. H
23. A
24. F
25. A
26. H
27. B
28. G
29. D
30. J
31. C
32. G
33. D
34. H
35. A
36. J
37. C
38. H
39. B
40. J

Answers: TerraNova Practice Test

Part 1

1. A
2. K
3. C
4. J
5. C
6. G
7. C
8. G
9. C
10. H
11. B
12. H

Part 2

13. C
14. J
15. B
16. G
17. C
18. D
19. B
20. G
21. B
22. H
23. B
24. G
25. B
26. G
27. B
28. H
29. A
30. J
31. B
32. J
33. A
34. H
35. A
36. H
37. D
38. F
39. C
40. H
41. C
42. G
43. C
44. F
45. A

46. J
47. A
48. J
49. B
50. G
51. B
52. F
53. A
54. F
55. C
56. G

Part 3

1. A
2. H
3. D
4. H
5. E
6. F
7. C
8. G
9. B
10. G
11. D
12. H
13. B
14. J
15. D
16. H
17. B
18. G
19. C
20. H

Answer Sheet

1.	A	B	C	D		27.	A	B	C	D
2.	F	G	H	J		28.	F	G	H	J
3.	A	B	C	D		29.	A	B	C	D
4.	F	G	H	J		30.	F	G	H	J
5.	A	B	C	D		31.	A	B	C	D
6.	F	G	H	J		32.	F	G	H	J
7.	A	B	C	D		33.	A	B	C	D
8.	F	G	H	J		34.	F	G	H	J
9.	A	B	C	D		35.	A	B	C	D
10.	F	G	H	J		36.	F	G	H	J
11.	A	B	C	D		37.	A	B	C	D
12.	F	G	H	J		38.	F	G	H	J
13.	A	B	C	D		39.	A	B	C	D
14.	F	G	H	J		40.	F	G	H	J
15.	A	B	C	D		41.	A	B	C	D
16.	F	G	H	J		42.	F	G	H	J
17.	A	B	C	D		43.	A	B	C	D
18.	F	G	H	J		44.	F	G	H	J
19.	A	B	C	D		45.	A	B	C	D
20.	F	G	H	J		46.	F	G	H	J
21.	A	B	C	D		47.	A	B	C	D
22.	F	G	H	J		48.	F	G	H	J
23.	A	B	C	D		49.	A	B	C	D
24.	F	G	H	J		50.	F	G	H	J
25.	A	B	C	D		51	A	B	C	D
26.	F	G	H	J		52.	F	G	H	J

Blank Grids for Gridded Responses

1.

2.

3.

4.

5.

6.

7.

8.

9.

10.

11.

12.

Student Answer Sheet: NAEP Practice Test

Multiple Choice

1.	Ⓐ	Ⓑ	Ⓒ	Ⓓ	Ⓔ	27.	Ⓐ	Ⓑ	Ⓒ	Ⓓ	Ⓔ
2.	Ⓐ	Ⓑ	Ⓒ	Ⓓ	Ⓔ	28.	Ⓐ	Ⓑ	Ⓒ	Ⓓ	Ⓔ
3.	Ⓐ	Ⓑ	Ⓒ	Ⓓ	Ⓔ	29.	Ⓐ	Ⓑ	Ⓒ	Ⓓ	Ⓔ
4.	Ⓐ	Ⓑ	Ⓒ	Ⓓ	Ⓔ	30.	Ⓐ	Ⓑ	Ⓒ	Ⓓ	Ⓔ
5.	Ⓐ	Ⓑ	Ⓒ	Ⓓ	Ⓔ	31.	Ⓐ	Ⓑ	Ⓒ	Ⓓ	Ⓔ
6.	Ⓐ	Ⓑ	Ⓒ	Ⓓ	Ⓔ	32.	Ⓐ	Ⓑ	Ⓒ	Ⓓ	Ⓔ
7.	Ⓐ	Ⓑ	Ⓒ	Ⓓ	Ⓔ	33.	Ⓐ	Ⓑ	Ⓒ	Ⓓ	Ⓔ
8.	Ⓐ	Ⓑ	Ⓒ	Ⓓ	Ⓔ	34.	Ⓐ	Ⓑ	Ⓒ	Ⓓ	Ⓔ
9.	Ⓐ	Ⓑ	Ⓒ	Ⓓ	Ⓔ	35.	Ⓐ	Ⓑ	Ⓒ	Ⓓ	Ⓔ
10.	Ⓐ	Ⓑ	Ⓒ	Ⓓ	Ⓔ	36.	Ⓐ	Ⓑ	Ⓒ	Ⓓ	Ⓔ
11.	Ⓐ	Ⓑ	Ⓒ	Ⓓ	Ⓔ	37.	Ⓐ	Ⓑ	Ⓒ	Ⓓ	Ⓔ
12.	Ⓐ	Ⓑ	Ⓒ	Ⓓ	Ⓔ	38.	Ⓐ	Ⓑ	Ⓒ	Ⓓ	Ⓔ
13.	Ⓐ	Ⓑ	Ⓒ	Ⓓ	Ⓔ	39.	Ⓐ	Ⓑ	Ⓒ	Ⓓ	Ⓔ
14.	Ⓐ	Ⓑ	Ⓒ	Ⓓ	Ⓔ	40.	Ⓐ	Ⓑ	Ⓒ	Ⓓ	Ⓔ
15.	Ⓐ	Ⓑ	Ⓒ	Ⓓ	Ⓔ	41.	Ⓐ	Ⓑ	Ⓒ	Ⓓ	Ⓔ
16.	Ⓐ	Ⓑ	Ⓒ	Ⓓ	Ⓔ	42.	Ⓐ	Ⓑ	Ⓒ	Ⓓ	Ⓔ
17.	Ⓐ	Ⓑ	Ⓒ	Ⓓ	Ⓔ	43.	Ⓐ	Ⓑ	Ⓒ	Ⓓ	Ⓔ
18.	Ⓐ	Ⓑ	Ⓒ	Ⓓ	Ⓔ	44.	Ⓐ	Ⓑ	Ⓒ	Ⓓ	Ⓔ
19.	Ⓐ	Ⓑ	Ⓒ	Ⓓ	Ⓔ	45.	Ⓐ	Ⓑ	Ⓒ	Ⓓ	Ⓔ
20.	Ⓐ	Ⓑ	Ⓒ	Ⓓ	Ⓔ	46.	Ⓐ	Ⓑ	Ⓒ	Ⓓ	Ⓔ
21.	Ⓐ	Ⓑ	Ⓒ	Ⓓ	Ⓔ	47.	Ⓐ	Ⓑ	Ⓒ	Ⓓ	Ⓔ
22.	Ⓐ	Ⓑ	Ⓒ	Ⓓ	Ⓔ	48.	Ⓐ	Ⓑ	Ⓒ	Ⓓ	Ⓔ
23.	Ⓐ	Ⓑ	Ⓒ	Ⓓ	Ⓔ	49.	Ⓐ	Ⓑ	Ⓒ	Ⓓ	Ⓔ
24.	Ⓐ	Ⓑ	Ⓒ	Ⓓ	Ⓔ	50.	Ⓐ	Ⓑ	Ⓒ	Ⓓ	Ⓔ
25.	Ⓐ	Ⓑ	Ⓒ	Ⓓ	Ⓔ	51.	Ⓐ	Ⓑ	Ⓒ	Ⓓ	Ⓔ
26.	Ⓐ	Ⓑ	Ⓒ	Ⓓ	Ⓔ	52.	Ⓐ	Ⓑ	Ⓒ	Ⓓ	Ⓔ

Go On

Student Answer Sheet: NAEP Practice Test (continued)

53.	Ⓐ	Ⓑ	Ⓒ	Ⓓ	Ⓔ
54.	Ⓐ	Ⓑ	Ⓒ	Ⓓ	Ⓔ
55.	Ⓐ	Ⓑ	Ⓒ	Ⓓ	Ⓔ
56.	Ⓐ	Ⓑ	Ⓒ	Ⓓ	Ⓔ
57.	Ⓐ	Ⓑ	Ⓒ	Ⓓ	Ⓔ
58.	Ⓐ	Ⓑ	Ⓒ	Ⓓ	Ⓔ
59.	Ⓐ	Ⓑ	Ⓒ	Ⓓ	Ⓔ
60.	Ⓐ	Ⓑ	Ⓒ	Ⓓ	Ⓔ
61.	Ⓐ	Ⓑ	Ⓒ	Ⓓ	Ⓔ
62.	Ⓐ	Ⓑ	Ⓒ	Ⓓ	Ⓔ
63.	Ⓐ	Ⓑ	Ⓒ	Ⓓ	Ⓔ

Short Constructed Response

64. Short Constructed Response

65. Short Constructed Response

66. Short Constructed Response

67. Short Constructed Response

Extended Constructed Response

68. Extended Constructed Response

69. Extended Constructed Response

70. Extended Constructed Response

Student Answer Sheet: SAT 10 Practice Test

Mathematics: Problem Solving

1.	Ⓐ	Ⓑ	Ⓒ	Ⓓ
2.	Ⓕ	Ⓖ	Ⓗ	Ⓙ
3.	Ⓐ	Ⓑ	Ⓒ	Ⓓ
4.	Ⓕ	Ⓖ	Ⓗ	Ⓙ
5.	Ⓐ	Ⓑ	Ⓒ	Ⓓ
6.	Ⓕ	Ⓖ	Ⓗ	Ⓙ
7.	Ⓐ	Ⓑ	Ⓒ	Ⓓ
8.	Ⓕ	Ⓖ	Ⓗ	Ⓙ
9.	Ⓐ	Ⓑ	Ⓒ	Ⓓ
10.	Ⓕ	Ⓖ	Ⓗ	Ⓙ
11.	Ⓐ	Ⓑ	Ⓒ	Ⓓ
12.	Ⓕ	Ⓖ	Ⓗ	Ⓙ
13.	Ⓐ	Ⓑ	Ⓒ	Ⓓ
14.	Ⓕ	Ⓖ	Ⓗ	Ⓙ
15.	Ⓐ	Ⓑ	Ⓒ	Ⓓ
16.	Ⓕ	Ⓖ	Ⓗ	Ⓙ
17.	Ⓐ	Ⓑ	Ⓒ	Ⓓ
18.	Ⓕ	Ⓖ	Ⓗ	Ⓙ
19.	Ⓐ	Ⓑ	Ⓒ	Ⓓ
20.	Ⓕ	Ⓖ	Ⓗ	Ⓙ
21.	Ⓐ	Ⓑ	Ⓒ	Ⓓ
22.	Ⓕ	Ⓖ	Ⓗ	Ⓙ
23.	Ⓐ	Ⓑ	Ⓒ	Ⓓ
24.	Ⓕ	Ⓖ	Ⓗ	Ⓙ
25.	Ⓐ	Ⓑ	Ⓒ	Ⓓ

26.	Ⓕ	Ⓖ	Ⓗ	Ⓙ
27.	Ⓐ	Ⓑ	Ⓒ	Ⓓ
28.	Ⓕ	Ⓖ	Ⓗ	Ⓙ
29.	Ⓐ	Ⓑ	Ⓒ	Ⓓ
30.	Ⓕ	Ⓖ	Ⓗ	Ⓙ
31.	Ⓐ	Ⓑ	Ⓒ	Ⓓ
32.	Ⓕ	Ⓖ	Ⓗ	Ⓙ
33.	Ⓐ	Ⓑ	Ⓒ	Ⓓ
34.	Ⓕ	Ⓖ	Ⓗ	Ⓙ
35.	Ⓐ	Ⓑ	Ⓒ	Ⓓ
36.	Ⓕ	Ⓖ	Ⓗ	Ⓙ
37.	Ⓐ	Ⓑ	Ⓒ	Ⓓ
38.	Ⓕ	Ⓖ	Ⓗ	Ⓙ
39.	Ⓐ	Ⓑ	Ⓒ	Ⓓ
40.	Ⓕ	Ⓖ	Ⓗ	Ⓙ
41.	Ⓐ	Ⓑ	Ⓒ	Ⓓ
42.	Ⓕ	Ⓖ	Ⓗ	Ⓙ
43.	Ⓐ	Ⓑ	Ⓒ	Ⓓ
44.	Ⓕ	Ⓖ	Ⓗ	Ⓙ
45.	Ⓐ	Ⓑ	Ⓒ	Ⓓ
46.	Ⓕ	Ⓖ	Ⓗ	Ⓙ
47.	Ⓐ	Ⓑ	Ⓒ	Ⓓ
48.	Ⓕ	Ⓖ	Ⓗ	Ⓙ
49.	Ⓐ	Ⓑ	Ⓒ	Ⓓ
50.	Ⓕ	Ⓖ	Ⓗ	Ⓙ

Go On

Student Answer Sheet: SAT 10 Practice Test (continued)

Mathematics: Procedures

1. Ⓐ Ⓑ Ⓒ Ⓓ Ⓔ
2. Ⓕ Ⓖ Ⓗ Ⓙ Ⓚ
3. Ⓐ Ⓑ Ⓒ Ⓓ Ⓔ
4. Ⓕ Ⓖ Ⓗ Ⓙ Ⓚ
5. Ⓐ Ⓑ Ⓒ Ⓓ Ⓔ
6. Ⓕ Ⓖ Ⓗ Ⓙ Ⓚ
7. Ⓐ Ⓑ Ⓒ Ⓓ Ⓔ
8. Ⓕ Ⓖ Ⓗ Ⓙ Ⓚ
9. Ⓐ Ⓑ Ⓒ Ⓓ Ⓔ
10. Ⓕ Ⓖ Ⓗ Ⓙ Ⓚ
11. Ⓐ Ⓑ Ⓒ Ⓓ Ⓔ
12. Ⓕ Ⓖ Ⓗ Ⓙ Ⓚ
13. Ⓐ Ⓑ Ⓒ Ⓓ Ⓔ
14. Ⓕ Ⓖ Ⓗ Ⓙ Ⓚ
15. Ⓐ Ⓑ Ⓒ Ⓓ Ⓔ

16. Ⓕ Ⓖ Ⓗ Ⓙ Ⓚ
17. Ⓐ Ⓑ Ⓒ Ⓓ Ⓔ
18. Ⓕ Ⓖ Ⓗ Ⓙ Ⓚ
19. Ⓐ Ⓑ Ⓒ Ⓓ Ⓔ
20. Ⓕ Ⓖ Ⓗ Ⓙ Ⓚ
21. Ⓐ Ⓑ Ⓒ Ⓓ Ⓔ
22. Ⓕ Ⓖ Ⓗ Ⓙ Ⓚ
23. Ⓐ Ⓑ Ⓒ Ⓓ Ⓔ
24. Ⓕ Ⓖ Ⓗ Ⓙ Ⓚ
25. Ⓐ Ⓑ Ⓒ Ⓓ Ⓔ
26. Ⓕ Ⓖ Ⓗ Ⓙ Ⓚ
27. Ⓐ Ⓑ Ⓒ Ⓓ Ⓔ
28. Ⓕ Ⓖ Ⓗ Ⓙ Ⓚ
29. Ⓐ Ⓑ Ⓒ Ⓓ Ⓔ
30. Ⓕ Ⓖ Ⓗ Ⓙ Ⓚ

Student Answer Sheet: ITBS Practice Test

Multiple Choice

1.	Ⓐ	Ⓑ	Ⓒ	Ⓓ
2.	Ⓕ	Ⓖ	Ⓗ	Ⓙ
3.	Ⓐ	Ⓑ	Ⓒ	Ⓓ
4.	Ⓕ	Ⓖ	Ⓗ	Ⓙ
5.	Ⓐ	Ⓑ	Ⓒ	Ⓓ
6.	Ⓕ	Ⓖ	Ⓗ	Ⓙ
7.	Ⓐ	Ⓑ	Ⓒ	Ⓓ
8.	Ⓕ	Ⓖ	Ⓗ	Ⓙ
9.	Ⓐ	Ⓑ	Ⓒ	Ⓓ
10.	Ⓕ	Ⓖ	Ⓗ	Ⓙ
11.	Ⓐ	Ⓑ	Ⓒ	Ⓓ
12.	Ⓕ	Ⓖ	Ⓗ	Ⓙ
13.	Ⓐ	Ⓑ	Ⓒ	Ⓓ
14.	Ⓕ	Ⓖ	Ⓗ	Ⓙ
15.	Ⓐ	Ⓑ	Ⓒ	Ⓓ
16.	Ⓕ	Ⓖ	Ⓗ	Ⓙ
17.	Ⓐ	Ⓑ	Ⓒ	Ⓓ
18.	Ⓕ	Ⓖ	Ⓗ	Ⓙ
19.	Ⓐ	Ⓑ	Ⓒ	Ⓓ
20.	Ⓕ	Ⓖ	Ⓗ	Ⓙ
21.	Ⓐ	Ⓑ	Ⓒ	Ⓓ
22.	Ⓕ	Ⓖ	Ⓗ	Ⓙ
23.	Ⓐ	Ⓑ	Ⓒ	Ⓓ
24.	Ⓕ	Ⓖ	Ⓗ	Ⓙ
25.	Ⓐ	Ⓑ	Ⓒ	Ⓓ
26.	Ⓕ	Ⓖ	Ⓗ	Ⓙ
27.	Ⓐ	Ⓑ	Ⓒ	Ⓓ
28.	Ⓕ	Ⓖ	Ⓗ	Ⓙ
29.	Ⓐ	Ⓑ	Ⓒ	Ⓓ
30.	Ⓕ	Ⓖ	Ⓗ	Ⓙ
31.	Ⓐ	Ⓑ	Ⓒ	Ⓓ
32.	Ⓕ	Ⓖ	Ⓗ	Ⓙ
33.	Ⓐ	Ⓑ	Ⓒ	Ⓓ
34.	Ⓕ	Ⓖ	Ⓗ	Ⓙ
35.	Ⓐ	Ⓑ	Ⓒ	Ⓓ
36.	Ⓕ	Ⓖ	Ⓗ	Ⓙ
37.	Ⓐ	Ⓑ	Ⓒ	Ⓓ
38.	Ⓕ	Ⓖ	Ⓗ	Ⓙ
39.	Ⓐ	Ⓑ	Ⓒ	Ⓓ
40.	Ⓕ	Ⓖ	Ⓗ	Ⓙ

Student Answer Sheet: TerraNova Practice Test

Part 1

1. Ⓐ Ⓑ Ⓒ Ⓓ Ⓔ
2. Ⓕ Ⓖ Ⓗ Ⓙ Ⓚ
3. Ⓐ Ⓑ Ⓒ Ⓓ Ⓔ
4. Ⓕ Ⓖ Ⓗ Ⓙ Ⓚ
5. Ⓐ Ⓑ Ⓒ Ⓓ Ⓔ
6. Ⓕ Ⓖ Ⓗ Ⓙ Ⓚ
7. Ⓐ Ⓑ Ⓒ Ⓓ Ⓔ
8. Ⓕ Ⓖ Ⓗ Ⓙ
9. Ⓐ Ⓑ Ⓒ Ⓓ
10. Ⓕ Ⓖ Ⓗ Ⓙ
11. Ⓐ Ⓑ Ⓒ Ⓓ
12. Ⓕ Ⓖ Ⓗ Ⓙ
13. Ⓐ Ⓑ Ⓒ Ⓓ
14. Ⓕ Ⓖ Ⓗ Ⓙ
15. Ⓐ Ⓑ Ⓒ Ⓓ
16. Ⓕ Ⓖ Ⓗ Ⓙ
17. Ⓐ Ⓑ Ⓒ Ⓓ

Part 2

18. Ⓕ Ⓖ Ⓗ Ⓙ
19. Ⓐ Ⓑ Ⓒ Ⓓ
20. Ⓕ Ⓖ Ⓗ Ⓙ
21. Ⓐ Ⓑ Ⓒ Ⓓ
22. Ⓕ Ⓖ Ⓗ Ⓙ
23. Ⓐ Ⓑ Ⓒ Ⓓ
24. Ⓕ Ⓖ Ⓗ Ⓙ
25. Ⓐ Ⓑ Ⓒ Ⓓ
26. Ⓕ Ⓖ Ⓗ Ⓙ
27. Ⓐ Ⓑ Ⓒ Ⓓ
28. Ⓕ Ⓖ Ⓗ Ⓙ

29. Ⓐ Ⓑ Ⓒ Ⓓ
30. Ⓕ Ⓖ Ⓗ Ⓙ
31. Ⓐ Ⓑ Ⓒ Ⓓ
32. Ⓕ Ⓖ Ⓗ Ⓙ
33. Ⓐ Ⓑ Ⓒ Ⓓ
34. Ⓕ Ⓖ Ⓗ Ⓙ
35. Ⓐ Ⓑ Ⓒ Ⓓ
36. Ⓕ Ⓖ Ⓗ Ⓙ
37. Ⓐ Ⓑ Ⓒ Ⓓ
38. Ⓕ Ⓖ Ⓗ Ⓙ
39. Ⓐ Ⓑ Ⓒ Ⓓ
40. Ⓕ Ⓖ Ⓗ Ⓙ
41. Ⓐ Ⓑ Ⓒ Ⓓ
42. Ⓕ Ⓖ Ⓗ Ⓙ
43. Ⓐ Ⓑ Ⓒ Ⓓ
44. Ⓕ Ⓖ Ⓗ Ⓙ
45. Ⓐ Ⓑ Ⓒ Ⓓ
46. Ⓕ Ⓖ Ⓗ Ⓙ
47. Ⓐ Ⓑ Ⓒ Ⓓ
48. Ⓕ Ⓖ Ⓗ Ⓙ
49. Ⓐ Ⓑ Ⓒ Ⓓ
50. Ⓕ Ⓖ Ⓗ Ⓙ
51. Ⓐ Ⓑ Ⓒ Ⓓ
52. Ⓕ Ⓖ Ⓗ Ⓙ
53. Ⓐ Ⓑ Ⓒ Ⓓ
54. Ⓕ Ⓖ Ⓗ Ⓙ
55. Ⓐ Ⓑ Ⓒ Ⓓ
56. Ⓕ Ⓖ Ⓗ Ⓙ

Go On

Student Answer Sheet: TerraNova Practice Test
(continued)

Part 3

1. Ⓐ Ⓑ Ⓒ Ⓓ Ⓔ
2. Ⓕ Ⓖ Ⓗ Ⓙ Ⓚ
3. Ⓐ Ⓑ Ⓒ Ⓓ Ⓔ
4. Ⓕ Ⓖ Ⓗ Ⓙ Ⓚ
5. Ⓐ Ⓑ Ⓒ Ⓓ Ⓔ
6. Ⓕ Ⓖ Ⓗ Ⓙ Ⓚ
7. Ⓐ Ⓑ Ⓒ Ⓓ Ⓔ
8. Ⓕ Ⓖ Ⓗ Ⓙ Ⓚ
9. Ⓐ Ⓑ Ⓒ Ⓓ Ⓔ
10. Ⓕ Ⓖ Ⓗ Ⓙ Ⓚ
11. Ⓐ Ⓑ Ⓒ Ⓓ Ⓔ
12. Ⓕ Ⓖ Ⓗ Ⓙ Ⓚ
13. Ⓐ Ⓑ Ⓒ Ⓓ Ⓔ
14. Ⓕ Ⓖ Ⓗ Ⓙ Ⓚ
15. Ⓐ Ⓑ Ⓒ Ⓓ Ⓔ
16. Ⓕ Ⓖ Ⓗ Ⓙ Ⓚ
17. Ⓐ Ⓑ Ⓒ Ⓓ Ⓔ
18. Ⓕ Ⓖ Ⓗ Ⓙ Ⓚ
19. Ⓐ Ⓑ Ⓒ Ⓓ Ⓔ
20. Ⓕ Ⓖ Ⓗ Ⓙ Ⓚ